The Guardian

QUICK CROSSWORDS BOOK 2

Published in 2022 by Welbeck
an imprint of Welbeck Non-Fiction,
part of Welbeck Publishing Group
Based in London and Sydney
www.welbeckpublishing.com

Editorial: Ben McConnell and Millie Acers
Design: Bauer Media and Eliana Holder

A CIP catalogue for this book is available from the British
Library.

ISBN: 978-1-80279-105-1

Printed in the United Kingdom

10 9 8 7 6 5 4 3 2 1

The Guardian

QUICK CROSSWORDS ^{BOOK} 2

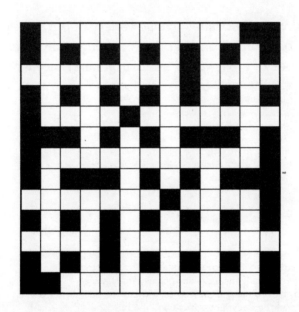

A compilation of more than **200**
enjoyable puzzles

WELBECK

About the Guardian

The *Guardian* has published honest and fearless journalism, free from commercial or political interference, since it was founded in 1821.

It now also publishes a huge variety of puzzles every day, both online and in print, covering many different types of crosswords, sudoku, general knowledge quizzes and more.

Introduction

Welcome to the second book in the *Guardian*'s challenging puzzle series. The humble quick crossword puzzle has appeared in the pages of the *Guardian* for decades, and these crosswords have been curated especially from recent issues to form a bumper batch of pure enjoyment.

These crosswords are designed to be solvable in a short time – there are not mountains of clues to work through. However, they are not easy. While a crossword expert may be able to solve them in a single break in the day, it is much more likely that you will have to step away and return to them later. Try it – your mind has a pleasantly surprising way of working on the answers without you even knowing.

Above all though, please enjoy this book! The world is full of challenges, but we hope that these challenges will provide a delightful diversion for you.

1

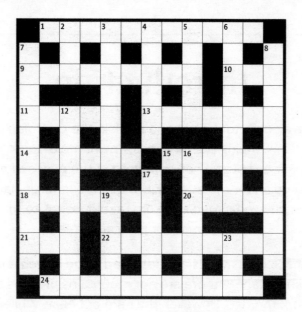

ACROSS

1 Stringed instruments (5,6)
9 Oil (9)
10 Watering hole (3)
11 Arrest (5)
13 Experiencing nausea when being driven (7)
14 Tartan cloths (6)
15 Decree (6)
18 Closely ranked crowd of people (7)
20 Fantastic but vain hope (5)
21 Muslim religious festival (3)
22 Large and important church (9)
24 Put behind bars (11)

DOWN

2 Take something without the owner's consent (3)
3 Made a sound like a horse (7)
4 Swagger (6)
5 Make different (5)
6 Stubborn (9)
7 Condiment made by grinding dried unripe berries together with their husks (5,6)
8 Beasts of burden (4,7)
12 Public space serving scones and cream etc (3,6)
16 Common European and Asian hoofed grazing animals (3,4)
17 Unusual and interesting (6)
19 Ghanaian capital (5)
23 Decomposition (3)

Solution see page 233

2

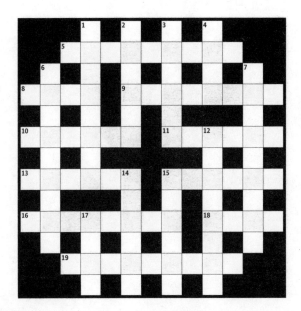

ACROSS

5 Target of abuse (4,5)

8 Tie (4)

9 Fine thread (8)

10 Keep several things going at the same time (6)

11 Style of hat for a woman (6)

13 Buddhist chant (6)

15 Someone who finds pleasure in hurting others (6)

16 Unexpected piece of good luck (8)

18 Hang over, menacingly (4)

19 Large hoofed animal with a very thick skin (9)

DOWN

1 Work extra hard to achieve something (4,1,3)

2 Smother — suppress (6)

3 Characteristic of the French (6)

4 Much valued — fruit (4)

6 Using compressed air (9)

7 In a difficult situation? (2,3,4)

12 US flag (3,5)

14 Indifference (6)

15 Food dishes, often tossed and dressed (6)

17 Take a gun from its holster (4)

Solution see page 233

3

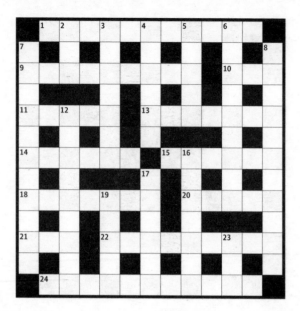

ACROSS

1 Exceptionally good (11)
9 Exceed in figures (9)
10 In the past (3)
11 Honest (abbr) (5)
13 Dried up (7)
14 Nice country! (6)
15 Cuban cigar (6)
18 Posh milliner or dressmaker (7)
20 Person of beauty, purity or kindness? (5)
21 Saucer in the sky? (3)
22 Monstrous sea creature (9)
24 Underwater bomb (5,6)

DOWN

2 Tedious routine (3)
3 Harsh — corrosive (7)
4 Human joints (6)
5 City in south-west Spain, famous for sherry (5)
6 Shackled workers? (5,4)
7 Known globally (5-6)
8 Touting for business without an appointment (4-7)
12 Pretentiously imposing — organised (anag) (9)
16 Confederate state during the American Civil War (7)
17 Relating to the large bony frame at the base of a human spine (6)
19 Discontinue a relationship (5)
23 Take more than one's share (3)

Solution see page 233

4

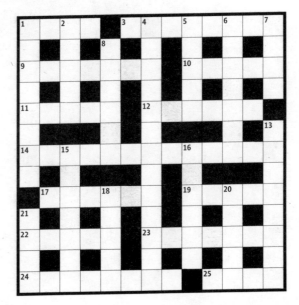

ACROSS

1 Belch (4)

3 Top (8)

9 Alter to improve appearance (5,2)

10 Restorative (5)

11 Recurrent unifying idea (5)

12 Burdensome (6)

14 Men only get-together (8,5)

17 Scientist (6)

19 Czech dance (5)

22 Male partner (5)

23 Boastful display (7)

24 Exploding shell fragments (8)

25 Exclamation of excitement when going fast (4)

DOWN

1 Moveable containers for washing the body (8)

2 Cheek cosmetic (5)

4 (Of a book) totally engrossing (13)

5 Milky fluid from poppies, rubber plants etc (5)

6 Wine seller (7)

7 Loose scrum (4)

8 Steal (6)

13 Tree with winged seeds (8)

15 Jemmy (7)

16 Tree of north temperate regions, with flowers borne in catkins (6)

18 Greasy breakfast? (3-2)

20 Restraint on a dog? (5)

21 Causes underlying an action or situation (4)

Solution see page 233

5

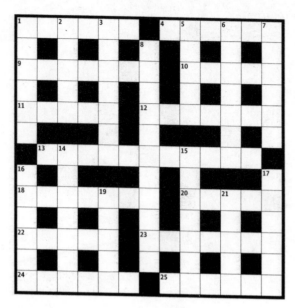

ACROSS

1 Rye, for example (6)
4 Ghost — pluck (6)
9 Capital of Andalusia (7)
10 Paved area next to a house (5)
11 Large truck (5)
12 Abdominal organs — cars vie (anag) (7)
13 Alfresco social event (6,5)
18 Take revenge (3,4)
20 Dark brown fur (5)
22 Fix software glitches (5)
23 Anxious (7)
24 Without forethought (6)
25 Without shoes (6)

DOWN

1 Fortified building (6)
2 Vehicle driven remotely over extraterrestrial terrain (5)
3 Assuaged (7)
5 Heads of the Roman Catholic Church (5)
6 Forward a message on a microblog website (7)
7 Involving movement in either direction (3–3)
8 It's anyone's guess (6,5)
14 French Riviera resort (7)
15 Loser (4–3)
16 Moroccan seaport (6)
17 Required (6)
19 Watch (5)
21 HMS Bounty's captain (5)

Solution see page 234

6

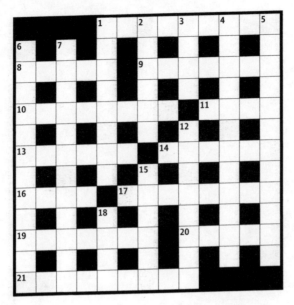

ACROSS

1 Adorn (9)
8 Precise (5)
9 Info (slang) — dishonourable (3-4)
10 Ragged (8)
11 Cheese-making by-product (4)
13 Provoke (6)
14 Northernmost town of mainland Britain (6)
16 Oversupply (4)
17 Final performance (4,4)
19 Elementary particle with zero charge (7)
20 Serving spoon (5)
21 Gas used in welding (9)

DOWN

1 Earnest plea (8)
2 Credence (6)
3 Grassed area (4)
4 Expressed differently (2,5,5)
5 Seductively persuasive — tough doyenne (anag) (5-7)
6 US state, capital Charleston (4,8)
7 Fashion house creations (5,7)
12 Hellenic (anag) — material (8)
15 Momentary pain (6)
18 Heehaw (4)

Solution see page 234

7

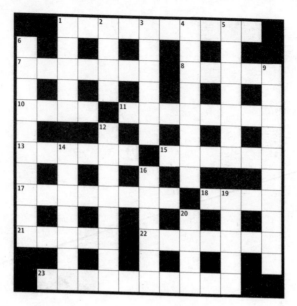

ACROSS

1 Exuberant (10)
7 Accuse of a wrong (7)
8 Firework (disappointing, if damp) (5)
10 Hairy Himalayan humanoid (4)
11 Move on water by standing on a board with a sail (8)
13 South American cowboy (6)
15 Biological catalyst (6)
17 Servitude (8)
18 Old Bill (slang) (4)
21 Careful user of a piggy bank? (5)
22 Refuse container (7)
23 Brass musical instrument (6,4)

DOWN

1 Incinerated (5)
2 Wading bird with a down-curved bill (4)
3 Game that depends on service (6)
4 Hotel guest staying for a prolonged period (8)
5 Montevideo's country (7)
6 Inflammation making it difficult to speak (10)
9 Neutral area between two rival powers (6,4)
12 Little ones (8)
14 Against the current (7)
16 Seat for passengers on the back of an elephant (6)
19 Citified (5)
20 European capital, known until 1924 as Christiania (4)

Solution see page 234

8

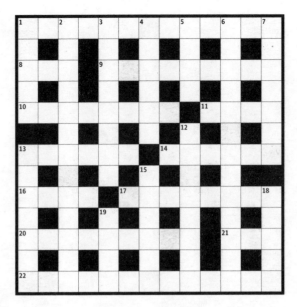

ACROSS

1 Dishonesty (13)
8 Mate (3)
9 Exposing human folly to ridicule (9)
10 Dedicated birdwatcher (8)
11 Floating navigation mark (4)
13 Long upholstered seat (6)
14 Advancing (6)
16 Figure skater's jump (4)
17 Look (cockney slang) — Smithfield workers (8)
20 Hardship (9)
21 Female sheep (3)
22 In an impressively beautiful manner (13)

DOWN

1 Storehouse (5)
2 Light exercises to promote general fitness (13)
3 Without others knowing (2,6)
4 Parent (6)
5 Bait (4)
6 Motivation (13)
7 Spread apart (7)
12 Settle firmly (8)
13 Clear off! (7)
15 Merger (6)
18 Shabby (5)
19 Become wearisome (4)

Solution see page 234

9

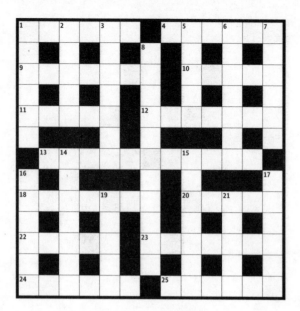

ACROSS

1 The 1960s, for example (6)
4 Arise (4,2)
9 Don Quixote's tongue (7)
10 Ivanhoe's creator (5)
11 Outmoded (5)
12 Error (7)
13 Add-ons (11)
18 Caribbean country (7)
20 Clique of plotters (5)
22 Four Quartets poet (5)
23 Made into a god (7)
24 Globe (6)
25 Spoon-bender Uri (6)

DOWN

1 Notorious French marquis, d. 1814 (2,4)
2 Intone (5)
3 Diminish — shrink slowly (7)
5 Baby's teething biscuits (5)
6 Bottled fuel (7)
7 Salesperson's talk (6)
8 Author of Under the Greenwood Tree (6,5)
14 Protect and care for lovingly (7)
15 Be recumbent (7)
16 Escape route (6)
17 Unpowered aircraft (6)
19 In motion — out of bed (5)
21 Fab — fish (5)

Solution see page 235

10

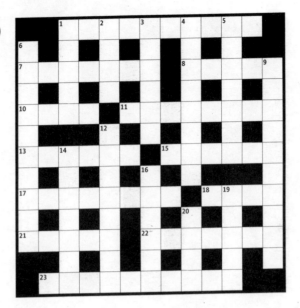

ACROSS

1 Resemblance (10)
7 Expression of approval (7)
8 Faint-hearted (5)
10 Board game (4)
11 Tyrannical ruler (8)
13 Affable (6)
15 Sausage in a bun (3,3)
17 Navy, army or air force unit (8)
18 Not fake news! (4)
21 Stout cotton cloth (5)
22 Become bankrupt (2,5)
23 Titular university head (10)

DOWN

1 Broken piece — London skyscraper (5)
2 Created (4)
3 Express oneself without restraint (3,3)
4 Turning (8)
5 Enticed (7)
6 Expressed regret for what one has done (10)
9 Showing a disrespectful attitude (10)
12 Stringed instrument, usually played with a plectrum (8)
14 Provide with materials for life and growth (7)
16 Stare wide-eyed in amazement (6)
19 Britain's only venomous snake (5)
20 Reduce the population by selective slaughter (4)

Solution see page 235

11

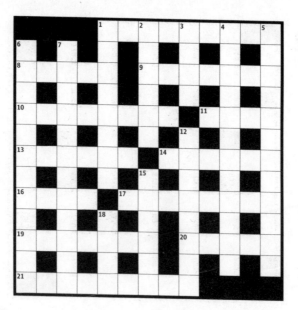

ACROSS

1 Press on (4,5)
8 Catchy phrases in pop songs (5)
9 Says yes (7)
10 Similarly (8)
11 Recommend strongly (4)
13 Famished (6)
14 Introductory textbook (6)
16 Ship used in the search for the Golden Fleece (4)
17 Discrepancy (8)
19 Malign — rude act (anag) (7)
20 Stitch up (5)
21 Scattering (9)

DOWN

1 Characters that gain one access? (8)
2 In short supply (6)
3 Annoyingly playful (4)
4 Data-based — inexpert male (anag) (12)
5 Crestfallen (12)
6 With enthusiastic devotion (12)
7 Mirror (7,5)
12 Rewarding (8)
15 Stroke (6)
18 Month (4)

Solution see page 235

12

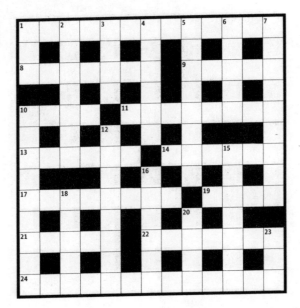

ACROSS

1 Rubella (6,7)
8 Newsworthy (7)
9 Made reference to — edict (anag) (5)
10 Top edge of a container (4)
11 Fidgety (8)
13 Cleric (6)
14 Make a discordant ringing noise (6)
17 Avoid (3,5)
19 Purchases (4)
21 With a forward motion (5)
22 Contrite (7)
24 Broke up (13)

DOWN

1 Intestines (3)
2 Reproduction (7)
3 Masonry construction for spanning an opening (4)
4 Fungal disease of plants (6)
5 Island in San Francisco Bay (8)
6 Flexible (5)
7 Avoids (9)
10 Person protecting a VIP (9)
12 Sledge (8)
15 Gastronome (7)
16 Draw into the lungs (6)
18 Implements used in one's job (5)
20 House cleaner (4)
23 Inoperative (3)

Solution see page 235

13

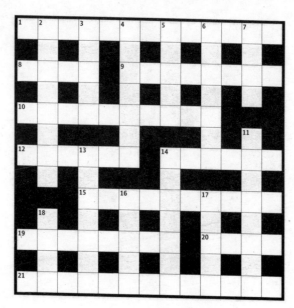

ACROSS

1 Work by Edward Lear? (8,5)
8 Actor in a principal role (4)
9 Characteristic of the time of the first four Hanoverian kings (8)
10 Staring in astonishment (6-4)
12 One-roomed apartment (6)
14 Repudiation (6)
15 High regard (10)
19 Got rid of (8)
20 Sore with a hard core and pus (4)
21 Continuing to look good (4-9)

DOWN

2 No longer in fashion (8)
3 Gesture of resignation (5)
4 Give little attention to (7)
5 Very dark black (5)
6 Encouraged (5,2)
7 Coarse tobacco (4)
11 Supporter of the deposed King James II (8)
13 Surgical instrument (7)
14 Ridicules (7)
16 Person given to quiet contemplation (5)
17 Roman river (5)
18 Prime number (4)

Solution see page 236

14

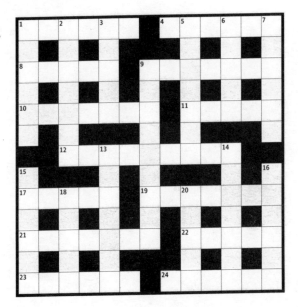

ACROSS

1 Hold spellbound (6)

4 Group of islands in the middle of the north Atlantic (6)

8 Ionian island (5)

9 Landlocked country, an Asian soviet before 1991, capital Yerevan (7)

10 Proportionately (3,4)

11 Remove from membership (5)

12 Smiling in an affected and silly way (9)

17 In myth, a plant whose fruit induced forgetfulness (5)

19 Group such as the Beatles (7)

21 Trace (7)

22 Imitative behaviour (5)

23 Position on a scale (6)

24 Riddle (6)

DOWN

1 Chef's instructions (6)

2 Of several different kinds (7)

3 Finnish steam bath (5)

5 Victoria Falls river (7)

6 Bowler's approach (3-2)

7 Basic commodity for which demand is constant (6)

9 Ballet pose on one leg (9)

13 Calling (7)

14 Cowardly (7)

15 Thin slice (6)

16 Horse that can go the distance (6)

18 The box (2,3)

20 Impure form of quartz, used as a gemstone (5)

Solution see page 236

15

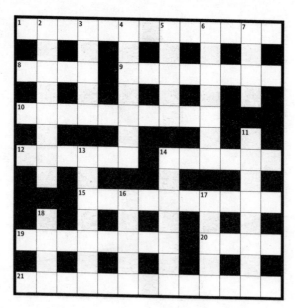

ACROSS

1 Bear of very little brain (6-3-4)
8 Respiratory organ (4)
9 Remorseful (8)
10 Make impure (10)
12 Baffles — projecting remnants (6)
14 Lab vessel (6)
15 Payment (for service rendered) (10)
19 Idle wanderer (8)
20 American athlete — Scottish soldier (4)
21 Pretending to be someone else (13)

DOWN

2 Flood (8)
3 ___ Mansell, 1992 F1 champion (5)
4 Put into words (7)
5 Hair dye (5)
6 One getting medical care (7)
7 Porcine sound (4)
11 Sparkling wine from Italy (8)
13 Kent seaside resort (7)
14 Islamic fast (7)
16 Wooden-soled shoes (5)
17 (Scottish or Irish) fool (5)
18 Old MacDonald's establishment (4)

Solution see page 236

16

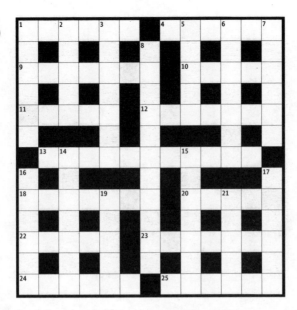

ACROSS

1 Top car (anag) — jailer (6)
4 Having existed from the beginning (6)
9 Conscientious (7)
10 Waits in hiding to attack (5)
11 Clean (anag) — weapon (5)
12 Outfit (7)
13 Having turrets and battlements (11)
18 It may be (7)
20 Freshwater fish (5)
22 Hazardous (5)
23 High — rapturous (7)
24 Enlarge (6)
25 In disagreement (2,4)

DOWN

1 Embrace (6)
2 Stage — hoax (3,2)
3 Unconventional (7)
5 Irritates (5)
6 Large tent (7)
7 Tied — beaten (6)
8 Banned from consideration (11)
14 Spray can (7)
15 Allure (7)
16 Treated mercifully (6)
17 British financier and coloniser in southern Africa, d. 1902 (6)
19 Up to now (2,3)
21 Famous (5)

Solution see page 236

17

ACROSS

1 White Anglo-Saxon Protestant (4)

3 Indonesian island, 1883 site of a huge volcanic eruption (8)

9 Officer of the royal household (7)

10 Ceasefire (5)

11 Sponge (5)

12 Period of greatest prosperity (6)

14 Artist like Edvard Munch (13)

17 Healthcare facility (6)

19 Thrown with force (5)

22 Increase speed (3,2)

23 Hostile attacks (7)

24 Of concern (8)

25 Witty remark (4)

DOWN

1 Unfortunate (8)

2 Calamari (5)

4 Drums etc (6,7)

5 Young domestic pet (5)

6 Destructive wave (7)

7 Lying between the sheets (4)

8 Get very cold (6)

13 Theatre scenery etc (5,3)

15 Prolonged fuss (7)

16 "… that sweet City with her dreaming spires …" (6)

18 A bit cold? (5)

20 Consumption (5)

21 Peak of a hill (4)

Solution see page 237

18

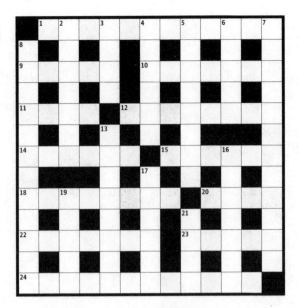

ACROSS

1 Someone on a short plank with wheels (12)
9 Spanish table wine (5)
10 Censure severely (7)
11 Cloying — repulsive (4)
12 Disease caused by vitamin B deficiency — ie briber (anag) (8)
14 Admirable — dignitary (6)
15 Tropical rainforest area (6)
18 After which (8)
20 City with a leaning tower (4)
22 In perfect circumstances (7)
23 Repeat the word(s) above (5)
24 Harlem basketball 17 (12)

DOWN

2 Door banger — detractor (7)
3 Piece on baby's bottle (4)
4 Dog? (6)
5 Decorative design made of one material sewn over another (8)
6 Continuous low-pitched note (5)
7 Cooler (12)
8 Systematic indoctrination (12)
13 Velvety fabric (8)
16 Cartilage (7)
17 Active sportsperson (6)
19 Set of beliefs (5)
21 Revise a text (4)

Solution see page 237

19

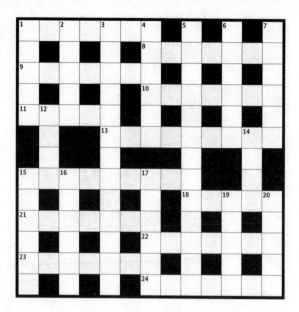

ACROSS

1 Moderate quantity (7)
8 In transit (French) (2,5)
9 Ireland's longest river (7)
10 Prolong (4,3)
11 Panache (5)
13 Now (9)
15 Sincerely intended with strong feeling (9)
18 Dolts (5)
21 Confused and empty talk (7)
22 River flowing from Colombia through Venezuela to the Atlantic (7)
23 Narrow-minded (7)
24 Vest (7)

DOWN

1 Hebrew prophet who led the Israelites on the Exodus (5)
2 Personal journal (5)
3 In turn (13)
4 Repairer (6)
5 Detailed artistic embellishment (13)
6 Erase — kill (3,3)
7 Not violently (6)
12 Remove (4)
14 Electrically charged (4)
15 1960s' dropout (6)
16 In the end (2,4)
17 Faults (6)
19 Seat without a back (5)
20 Inured to fatigue and hardship (5)

Solution see page 237

20

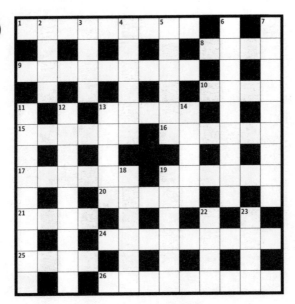

ACROSS

1 Medical practitioner (9)
8 Moderately cold (4)
9 Favour not available to all (9)
10 Oral exam (4)
13 Accommodation for prisoners (5)
15 Countless (6)
16 On the go (6)
17 Pleasure trip (6)
19 Wall paintings (6)
20 Old four-pence coin (5)
21 Inclined walkway (4)
24 Exaggerated (9)
25 US coin (4)
26 19th-century prime minister (9)

DOWN

2 Stringed instrument (4)
3 Set aside (4)
4 Pacified (6)
5 South-west African country, capital Luanda (6)
6 Murderous (9)
7 Awkward (3,2,4)
11 Government by one person with absolute power (9)
12 Spoken or written declaration (9)
13 Adhere (5)
14 Talent seeker (5)
18 Abase oneself (6)
19 Spoiled (6)
22 Not hilly (4)
23 The Ugly Duckling's outcome (4)

Solution see page 237

21

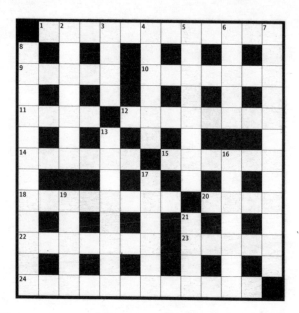

ACROSS

1 Contract (a disease) (4,4,4)
9 Thespian (5)
10 Tract of land (7)
11 Small island (4)
12 Where to pay before you leave (4,4)
14 Intensely passionate (6)
15 Container for burning incense (6)
18 Appealing to others (8)
20 Affirmative response (informal) (4)
22 Wipe out (7)
23 North-easterly US state (5)
24 Lethargy (12)

DOWN

2 In the open air (7)
3 Makes mistakes (4)
4 Relating to bone — so late (anag) (6)
5 Water between the UK and mainland Europe (5,3)
6 Representation (5)
7 Nose wiper (12)
8 Becomes a nun (5,3,4)
13 Untouched — spinet (8)
16 Taxonomic group whose members can interbreed (7)
17 Buries (6)
19 Opens wide (5)
21 Gulf sultanate (4)

Solution see page 238

22

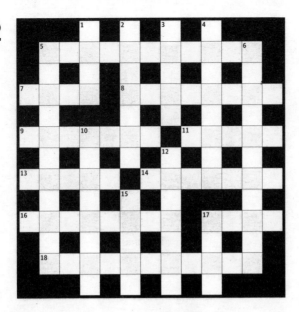

ACROSS

5 Pleasing to the ear (11)
7 Unpleasing to the eye (4)
8 Ta-ta (6-2)
9 Theft (7)
11 Data (5)
13 Female fox (5)
14 Eighth of a mile (7)
16 Predicted (8)
17 Shortly (4)
18 Given to pompous moralising (11)

DOWN

1 Gambit (4)
2 Far away (7)
3 Deluge (5)
4 Means of establishing who is present (4,4)
5 Generous (11)
6 Unpremeditated (11)
10 Capital of Wyoming (8)
12 One of a gang of English workmen destroying labour-saving mill machinery, 1811-16 (7)
15 Two-wheeled transport — was in low spirits (5)
17 Wintry precipitation (4)

Solution see page 238

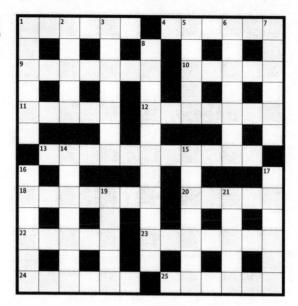

ACROSS

1 Fabric used for table linen (6)
4 Hey ___ ! (6)
9 Main packed group in a cycle race (7)
10 Short line at the end of the main strokes of a printed character (5)
11 About (Latin) (5)
12 Daft (7)
13 Book lover (11)
18 Dirty person or animal (7)
20 English physician and thesaurus compiler, d. 1869 (5)
22 Steam bath (5)
23 Concentrate (7)
24 Score (6)
25 Attic space (6)

DOWN

1 Describe in detail (6)
2 Chewer and grinder (5)
3 Leave port (3,4)
5 Take exam again (5)
6 Like a dream (7)
7 Stupid (6)
8 Protection from glare for winter sporters (4,7)
14 Drinks cooler? (3,4)
15 Hot paste used in North African cuisine — ass hair (anag) (7)
16 Counteract (6)
17 Motionless (2,4)
19 Large animal — objectionable person (5)
21 Someone beyond help (5)

Solution see page 238

24

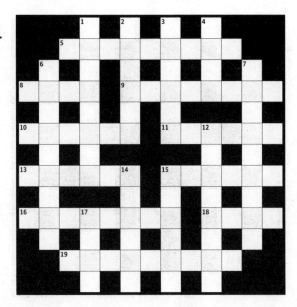

ACROSS

5 Stunningly beautiful (9)
8 Ring of light (4)
9 Very quickly (2,2,4)
10 Put to rights (6)
11 Wilfully divert something from its intended course (6)
13 Where maintenance items are kept (6)
15 Golfer's assistant (6)
16 Went to bed (6,2)
18 Garish (4)
19 State of being contented (9)

DOWN

1 Wrecker — sour beat (anag) (8)
2 Spread negative information about (6)
3 Made pathetic complaints (6)
4 Biting insect (4)
6 Bring a contentious matter to resolution (4,2,3)
7 Desiring success (9)
12 Strongly suggestive (of) (8)
14 Impose a task on — assign responsibility for (6)
15 Nut of the horse chestnut tree (6)
17 Christmas (4)

Solution see page 238

25

ACROSS

1 Government official (10)
7 Relaxing (7)
8 Cotton thread or fabric (5)
10 Unhurried (4)
11 Awning (8)
13 Eat like a bird —
   packet (anag) (4,2)
15 Spare tyre (6)
17 Shy (8)
18 Layout drawing (4)
21 Place frequently visited (5)
22 Sink one's ship deliberately (7)
23 Inexorable (10)

DOWN

1 Sumo wrestling tournament (5)
2 Eurasian sandpiper —
   Australian fish (4)
3 Complete (3-3)
4 Salad dish based on shredded
   cabbage (8)
5 Choose not to vote (7)
6 Grump (10)
9 Impartial (4-6)
12 Belgian surrealist painter,
   d. 1967 (8)
14 Travel daily to work (7)
16 Piece of material used to
   strengthen a garment (6)
19 British sports and racing
   car manufacturer (5)
20 Silent (4)

Solution see page 239

26

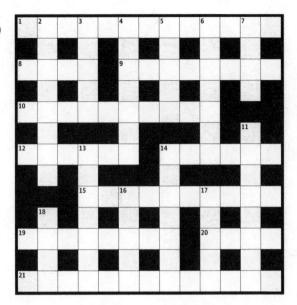

ACROSS

1 What's the big hurry? (6,3,4)
8 Unhappy (4)
9 Dutch gin (8)
10 Drowsiness (10)
12 Gentle breeze (6)
14 Well turned out (6)
15 Tactful (10)
19 Split up (8)
20 One-sided inclination (4)
21 Emotionally crushed (6-7)

DOWN

2 Ajar (4-4)
3 Norma (anag) — upright style of print (5)
4 Academic (7)
5 Was this the face that launch'd a thousand ships? (5)
6 Sudden outbreak of anger (5-2)
7 Journey (4)
11 Remove body hair (8)
13 Food fish (7)
14 Recklessly determined (2-2-3)
16 Hickory tree and its nut (5)
17 Fossilised resin used in jewellery (5)
18 Landing stage (4)

Solution see page 239

27

ACROSS

1 Dickens novel (6,5)
9 Recurring every eight years (9)
10 Auditory organ (3)
11 French military caps (5)
13 Motto under the Prince of Wales's feathers (German) (3,4)
14 Caribbean capital (6)
15 Loud piercing cry (6)
18 Square cap worn by Roman Catholic clergy (7)
20 Kilns for drying hops (5)
21 Industrious insect (3)
22 Hurry (4,5)
24 Love letters (7–4)

DOWN

2 Ignited (3)
3 Deer meat (7)
4 Dried grape (6)
5 Cambrian (5)
6 Samples (9)
7 Make things difficult for others (4,3,4)
8 Chess player of the highest class (11)
12 Operatic tenor, d. 2007 (9)
16 Dressed (7)
17 Small parcel (6)
19 Language of Sri Lanka (5)
23 Old French coin (3)

Solution see page 239

28

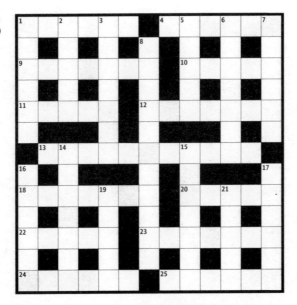

ACROSS

1 Type of fertiliser (6)

4 Free-for-all (6)

9 Sheep barber? (7)

10 Deliberate (5)

11 Something of just sentimental value (5)

12 Game played with 15 red balls, six of other colours and a white one (7)

13 Very discouraging (11)

18 Competitor (7)

20 Ages (5)

22 Volley (5)

23 Sap (7)

24 European city (with a Convention for commercial flying) (6)

25 Particular environment (6)

DOWN

1 Iranian language spoken in Afghanistan and Pakistan (6)

2 Make minor adjustments (5)

3 Make a crushing noise (7)

5 Literary lover (5)

6 An outstanding example of its kind! (7)

7 Irony — sarcasm (6)

8 Damaged by sub-zero cold (11)

14 North American pit viper (7)

15 Retail outlet for kids (7)

16 Playground equipment for kids (6)

17 Bloodsucking African fly (6)

19 Perfume (5)

21 Pointless (2,3)

Solution see page 239

29

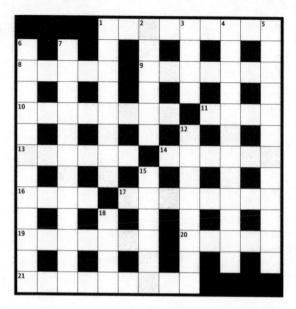

ACROSS

1 Medicated solution used for gargling (9)
8 Separated (5)
9 South African sun-dried meat (7)
10 Sudden occurrence (as of disease) (8)
11 In good health (4)
13 In poor health (6)
14 Low joints (6)
16 Prima donna (4)
17 Ancestor (8)
19 Young goose (7)
20 Stoneworker (5)
21 Fit to sail (9)

DOWN

1 Driving a car (8)
2 Cheerful — optimistic (6)
3 One of two equal parts (4)
4 Most especially (5,3,4)
5 Nervous and easily upset (6,6)
6 Common breakfast fare (5,3,4)
7 Spanish farewell (5,2,5)
12 Indecorous (8)
15 Looked for (6)
18 Relating to China (prefix) (4)

Solution see page 240

30

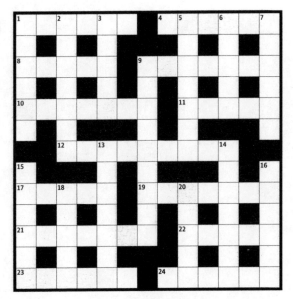

ACROSS

1 Small streams (6)
4 Declaration (6)
8 Framework of metal bars (5)
9 Fill with fear (7)
10 Refrain (7)
11 External (5)
12 Remiss (9)
17 Opening passage (abbr) (5)
19 Lufthansa, for example (7)
21 Long-lasting (7)
22 Prodded (5)
23 Reddish brown (6)
24 Cling (6)

DOWN

1 Ask for permission to be released (3,3)
2 Foreign letter — I'm no roc (anag) (7)
3 Dannii M's older sister (5)
5 Long-winded (7)
6 Card game for four (5)
7 Levels (6)
9 Stop (9)
13 Farewell (7)
14 Scintillate (7)
15 German Romantic songs for solo voice (6)
16 Interfere (6)
18 Mountain lakes (5)
20 Speedy (5)

Solution see page 240

31

ACROSS

1 Captivated (4)
3 Casino card game (8)
9 Suffocate (7)
10 Make available for sale (5)
11 Affray (5)
12 Sex (6)
14 Abstain from further action (5,2,2,4)
17 Close of play in cricket (6)
19 Watercourse (5)
22 Clumsy (5)
23 Contrary — inauspicious (7)
24 Selling aggressively (8)
25 Sleep in rough or improvised accommodation (4)

DOWN

1 Be like (8)
2 Slink after prey (5)
4 Perfectly OK (2,5,2,4)
5 Hit on the head (informal) (5)
6 Invigorate — her serf (anag) (7)
7 Sharp — acid (4)
8 Cunning scheme (informal) (6)
13 Completely naked (8)
15 Without guile (7)
16 Flourish (6)
18 Broken stone used in road-making (5)
20 Left-hand page (5)
21 Audible breath expressing weariness (4)

Solution see page 240

32

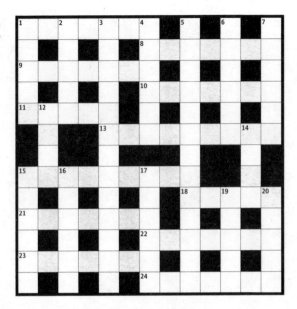

ACROSS

1 Shrub with drooping purple, red or white flowers (7)
8 Withdraw (4,3)
9 Pear-shaped fruit (7)
10 Resembling a big cat (7)
11 Martial art using split bamboo swords (5)
13 Skill in camping and related pursuits — card of two (anag) (9)
15 White ornamental stone (9)
18 Put off (5)
21 Pope (7)
22 Weak point (7)
23 Acknowledge defeat (7)
24 Intellectual (7)

DOWN

1 Without evasion (5)
2 Jester (5)
3 Opposition front bench (6,7)
4 US space project, 1960-72 (6)
5 Causing horror (5-8)
6 Peeping Tom's lady (6)
7 Bear witness (6)
12 Sinful (4)
14 Phoney (like news?) (4)
15 Characteristic to be considered (6)
16 Canvas cover over a shop entrance (6)
17 Sticky sweet (6)
19 Banal (5)
20 Unbending (5)

Solution see page 240

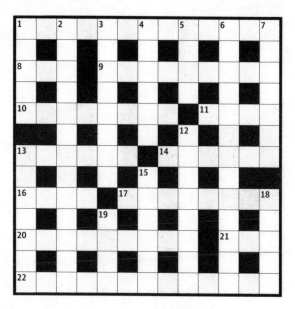

ACROSS

1 Small, pug-faced New England dog (6,7)

8 Informal information (3)

9 Designed for both mitts (3-6)

10 Bride or groom (8)

11 Continent (4)

13 Support — time (6)

14 Spectre — alcohol (6)

16 Small quantities of liquid (4)

17 Wrongly interprets text (8)

20 Role — nature (9)

21 Frozen water (3)

22 Dealt out again (13)

DOWN

1 Launch (5)

2 Advertisement carried up and down the street (8,5)

3 Away from the middle (8)

4 Sounded the horn (6)

5 Bring up (or back?) (4)

6 Businessman — I trail nudists (anag) (13)

7 Shining (7)

12 Meat on the bone served in barbecue sauce (5,3)

13 Motorbike passenger attachment (7)

15 Beer (6)

18 Tempo — drug (5)

19 Soviet Union's official news agency (4)

Solution see page 241

34

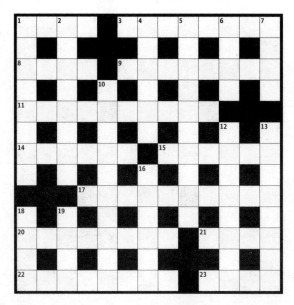

ACROSS

1 Endorse (4)
3 Buildings (8)
8 Exceedingly (4)
9 Sudden sharp increase in the birth rate (4,4)
11 Baker's tool (7,3)
14 Confused and slow to react (6)
15 Acrobatic feat — schisms (6)
17 Industrial city on the Ohio River (10)
20 Something difficult to say or understand (8)
21 Oral examination (4)
22 Divided — distinct (8)
23 Light toboggan (4)

DOWN

1 Liquid refreshment (8)
2 Set of musical bells (8)
4 ___ Reinhardt, French jazz guitarist, d. 1953 (6)
5 Unauthorised disposal of waste materials (3-7)
6 Wooden-soled shoe (4)
7 Japanese wrestling (4)
10 Colourful bird seen by streams and rivers (10)
12 Dessert — is it arum? (anag) (8)
13 Rough calculation (8)
16 Pronounce not guilty of criminal charges (6)
18 Old Testament prophet (4)
19 Witticism (4)

Solution see page 241

35

ACROSS

5 Tipper lorry (6,5)
7 Eye tooth (4)
8 Male hairdresser (8)
9 Success in a contest (7)
11 Piece of cloth for wiping eyes, nose etc (5)
13 Provocation (5)
14 Suffer when too hot (7)
16 Fighting on horseback in a tournament (8)
17 Lurch (4)
18 Don't tell! (4,3,4)

DOWN

1 Pleased with oneself (4)
2 Metal in thermometer or barometer (7)
3 Divest (5)
4 Fungus that discharges a cloud of spores when mature (8)
5 Chamber for entertaining guests (7,4)
6 Idiot — leaked chunk (anag) (11)
10 Trying (8)
12 Arrogant gait (7)
15 Pool to be won (5)
17 Black bird (4)

Solution see page 241

36

ACROSS

1 Harmful (11)
9 Invigorated (9)
10 Speak lovingly — cry softly (3)
11 Essential (5)
13 Refined and tasteful (7)
14 Bank employee (6)
15 Irish or Scottish accent? (6)
18 Pakistan's largest city (7)
20 Dig into (5)
21 Part of a fountain pen (3)
22 Serving food (7,2)
24 Dismissed peremptorily (4,7)

DOWN

2 Slippery swimmer (may be jellied) (3)
3 Rotate (7)
4 Repaired (6)
5 Slight push (5)
6 Highest ranking member of the celestial hierarchy (9)
7 Saying goodbye (5-6)
8 Awkward clash (11)
12 Bearable (9)
16 Anita ___ , Body Shop founder, d. 2007 (7)
17 Afternoon snooze (6)
19 Trainee officer (5)
23 Machine for separating cotton from its seeds (3)

Solution see page 241

37

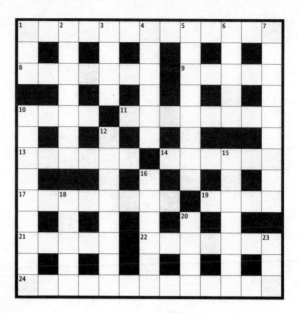

ACROSS

1 Vertical (13)
8 Spendthrift (7)
9 Fashions (5)
10 Turn (over) — impudent (4)
11,13 Aurora borealis (8,6)
14,17 Something quite extraordinary to look at (1,5,2,6)
19 Courageous (4)
21 Compare (5)
22 Coaster put under a glass (4,3)
24 Caused by mental pressure (6-7)

DOWN

1 Long church seat (3)
2 Lying down (7)
3 Be paid for work (4)
4 Small shapeless mass (6)
5 Unconscious (8)
6 Get stuck (5)
7 Vibrated sympathetically (9)
10 Legends (4,5)
12 Art prints (8)
15 Eyelet (7)
16 Engineless aircraft (6)
18 Hell's Angel? (5)
20 Little William (4)
23 Small amount (3)

Solution see page 242

38

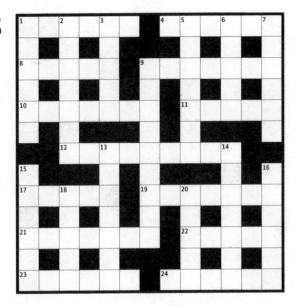

ACROSS

1 Cite as evidence (6)

4 Obliterate (6)

8 Brazilian dance (5)

9 Substance of which teeth are mainly composed (7)

10 Own up (7)

11 The way to get married in church? (5)

12 Fat (9)

17 Theme park attractions (5)

19 Individual performer (7)

21 Go on (7)

22 Small wood (5)

23 More than enough (6)

24 Limassol's island (6)

DOWN

1 French wine region (6)

2 Devilish (7)

3 Desist (5)

5 Short ceremonial tune for trumpets (7)

6 Goodbye to Spain (5)

7 County town and cathedral city of Devon (6)

9 Talked about (9)

13 Esteem (7)

14 Someone on an excursion (7)

15 Underpin (4,2)

16 Fish-eating mammals (6)

18 Male honeybee (5)

20 Fortunate (5)

Solution see page 242

39

ACROSS

1 Menu (4,2,4)
7 Master copy (8)
8 River port, capital of the Rhône department (4)
9 Thin strip of wood (4)
10 Enduring (7)
12 Sensational in appearance (11)
14 Increasing in magnitude (7)
16 European mountain range (4)
19 Bad smell (4)
20 Copycat (8)
21 Art Garfunkel song written for the 1978 animated film Watership Down — gets by hire (anag) (6,4)

DOWN

1 Gemstone (for Ms Bainbridge?) (5)
2 Beneficiary of a will (7)
3 Possesses (4)
4 Alternative plan for use, if necessary (8)
5 Annoyed (5)
6 Place where two streets meet (6)
11 Very attractive (8)
12 Moralising lecture (6)
13 Cradle song (7)
15 Bet (5)
17 Gunfire — attempts (5)
18 Tartan skirt (4)

Solution see page 242

40

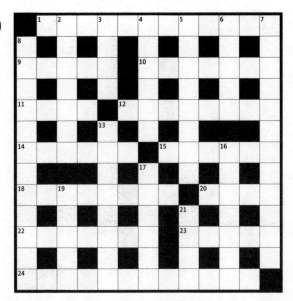

ACROSS

1 Drink alone in a pub? (4,2,3,3)
9 Distinguish oneself (5)
10 Naval officer (7)
11 Haircut (4)
12 Iconic theoretical physicist, d. 1955 (8)
14 Plump (6)
15 To do with mushrooms, say (6)
18 Reticent (8)
20 Cereal crop (4)
22 Close of day (7)
23 With everything counted (2,3)
24 Immediately (5,3,4)

DOWN

2 Proof of payment made (7)
3 Tow (4)
4 Unruffled (6)
5 Unsophisticated — posh menu (anag) (8)
6 Carried (5)
7 In an unceasingly intense way (12)
8 Depart hastily (4,1,7)
13 Pronto (2,1,5)
16 Author of Wind in the Willows (7)
17 Source (6)
19 Largest Greek island (5)
21 Sediment deposited by a river (4)

Solution see page 242

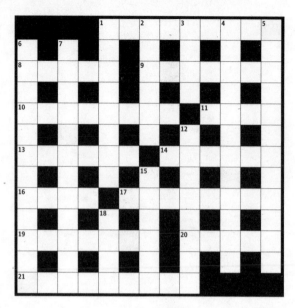

ACROSS

1 Type of piano (4,5)

8 Picked up by the ears? (5)

9 Berlin prison demolished in 1987 after the death of its last prisoner, Rudolf Hess (7)

10 Native American people, originally living in the Appalachian Mountains (8)

11 Willy Wonka's creator (4)

13 Beater (anag) — partial refund (6)

14 Bludgeoned (6)

16 Warty amphibian (4)

17 Scattered — irregular (8)

19 Uganda's capital (7)

20 Daniel ___ , American frontiersman, d. 1820 (5)

21 Magna Carta location (9)

DOWN

1 Malign (8)

2 Woven receptacle (6)

3 German tennis player, b. 1969 (4)

4 Critically ill (2,6,4)

5 Type of bus (6–6)

6 1960 Pinter play (3,9)

7 Aquatic bug (5,7)

12 Awful (8)

15 Drug such as morphine (6)

18 Boy's name — Indiana city (4)

42

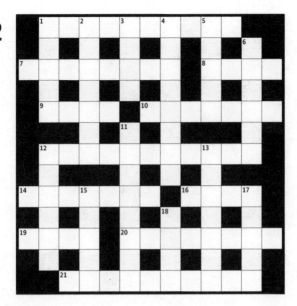

ACROSS

1 Liquid used in making soda bread — I'm Burt Kelt (anag) (10)

7 The Charge of the Light Brigade poet (8)

8 Stylishness (4)

9 Positive expectation (4)

10 Unexplained problem or fault (7)

12 Trickery (11)

14 Conciseness (7)

16 Birmingham (4)

19 Lively person — feasible idea (4)

20 Clandestine (4-4)

21 Hard round sweet (10)

DOWN

1 Deciduous tree with smooth grey bark (5)

2 Camping equipment (4,3)

3 Like a walk in the park? (4)

4 Musical scale — more inky (anag) (5,3)

5 Stand-in medic (5)

6 Subordinate (6)

11 Sticks for lame people (8)

12 Strip or small cube of fatty bacon (6)

13 Dirigible (7)

15 Large constellation — sign of the zodiac (5)

17 Stingy hoarder (5)

18 Court order restricting anti-social behaviour (4)

Solution see page 243

43

ACROSS

1 Small river fish (4)
3 Shocked (8)
9 Two-wheeled motor vehicle (7)
10 Frequently (5)
11 Correspond in sound (5)
12 Ridiculous (6)
14 Probably (2,6,2,3)
17 Complete agreement (6)
19 Lustrous globule prized as a gem (5)
22 Rotating machine tool (5)
23 Facilitates (7)
24 Circumspect (8)
25 Was in debt (4)

DOWN

1 Untidiness (8)
2 Sidekick (5)
4 Ignore — brush aside (4,1,5,3)
5 Accommodation (5)
6 In the fullness of time (5,2)
7 Hollow caused by a blow (4)
8 Run naked in public (6)
13 Employed — I led suit (anag) (8)
15 Cough medicine (7)
16 Heartfelt request — attraction (6)
18 Diaphanous (5)
20 Permit (5)
21 Haemorrhaged (4)

Solution see page 243

44

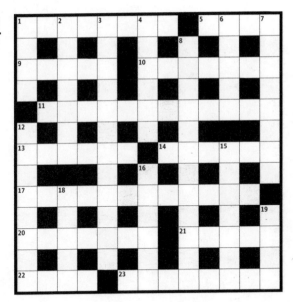

ACROSS

1 Item of bedroom furniture (8)
5 Done deeds (4)
9 Brilliant — deception (5)
10 Aerofoil at the back of a car to reduce lift at high speeds (7)
11 Countless (12)
13 Saudi Arabian capital (6)
14 Tic (6)
17 Sphere to be pocketed? (8,4)
20 Etc (3,2,2)
21 Drug used to treat Parkinson's disease (1-4)
22 Where the sun rises? (4)
23 Large bloodsucking insect (8)

DOWN

1 Child-bearing organ (4)
2 Years from 1811 to 1820 during George III's periods of insanity (7)
3 The only US president to have resigned from office (7,5)
4 Divide into two equal parts (6)
6 Star (5)
7 Harsh and shrill (8)
8 Owls by Belloc (anag) — severe gastroenteritis (12)
12 Card game scored with pegs (8)
15 Reprimand (4,3)
16 Wild bucking horse (6)
18 Solid (anag) — pools (5)
19 Shade of blue (4)

Solution see page 243

45

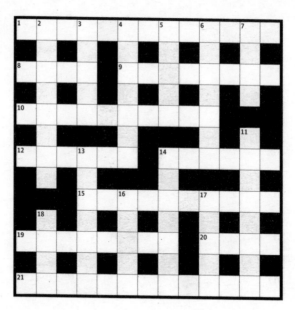

ACROSS

1 Slave to clothes labels (7,6)
8 Black marketeer (4)
9 Youth of the '50s and '60s wearing Edwardian–style clothes (5,3)
10 Sorcery skill (10)
12 Book of texts for the Catholic Mass (6)
14 Course set towards a selected point (6)
15 Where traffic is squeezed (10)
19 Formerly Abyssinia (8)
20 Was economical with the truth (4)
21 Radiation measurer (6,7)

DOWN

2 Frogs and toads (8)
3 Great destruction (5)
4 Relating to sight (7)
5 Spirit traditionally made from fermented grains or potatoes (5)
6 Type of crossword (7)
7 Metal that rusts (4)
11 Tangible (8)
13 Bro or sis (7)
14 Lava source (7)
16 Narrow down (5)
17 Hosiery material (5)
18 Infection of the eyelid (4)

Solution see page 244

46

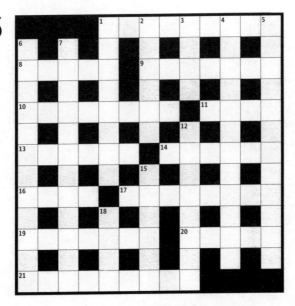

ACROSS

1 Showing calm self-control (9)
8 Tomorrow (or next week)? (5)
9 Wordy (7)
10 Spuds (8)
11 Ponder (4)
13 Obtain by threats (6)
14 Bavarian capital (6)
16 Object used on the set of a play (4)
17 Election campaigning (8)
19 Inhibit (7)
20 Body trunk (5)
21 Old county now divided into three (9)

DOWN

1 Line represented in black on the Tube map (8)
2 Inspection (6)
3 Lugholes (4)
4 Gradually developing (12)
5 Unexpectedly attract the most applause (5,3,4)
6 Overnight do for young girls (7,5)
7 Nazi Brownshirt (5,7)
12 Foreign dialogue translation shown on film (8)
15 Swiss breakfast? (6)
18 Dregs (4)

Solution see page 244

47

ACROSS

1 Mother superior (6)
4 Come again (5)
7 Full-frontal (4–2)
8 Wooden-framed instrument of execution (6)
9 Swelling of the eyelid (4)
10 Finland's capital (8)
12 Grow worse (11)
17 Divided skirt (8)
19 Run along easily (4)
20 Lay bare (6)
21 Fervid (6)
22 Gloss (5)
23 Filling food (6)

DOWN

1 Turned away (7)
2 Money owed that is unlikely to be repaid (3,4)
3 Seat of the Royal Military Academy (9)
4 Means of controlling a horse (5)
5 Committee of senior ministers (7)
6 Selling of goods to consumers (6)
11 Be quick! (4,5)
13 Oval shape (7)
14 Hinted (at) (7)
15 Cost (7)
16 Way in (6)
18 Undisputed world heavyweight champion, 1987 (5)

Solution see page 244

48

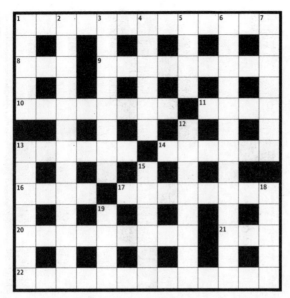

ACROSS

1 Carelessly lazy (13)
8 Saloon (3)
9 Impenitent (9)
10 Lively eagerness (8)
11 Bog (4)
13 Wicked (6)
14 Celebrations (6)
16 Harvest (4)
17 Deficiency (8)
20 New and old parts of the Bible (9)
21 Anger (3)
22 Conker (5,8)

DOWN

1 Sign of the zodiac (5)
2 Preliminary event (7–6)
3 Marine museum (8)
4 Modifies (6)
5 Central London district (4)
6 Sympathy (13)
7 Paying guests (7)
12 Rubbish — it rusted (anag) (8)
13 Score a surface (7)
15 Extract grain from husks (6)
18 Put up (5)
19 Narrow road (4)

Solution see page 244

49

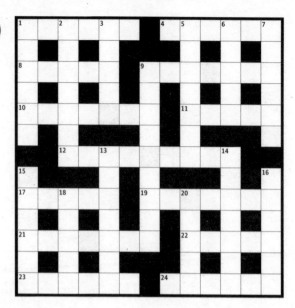

ACROSS

1 Sorrowful through loss (6)
4 Snooker rest (6)
8 Replete (5)
9 Let the cat out of the bag (7)
10 Ineffective (7)
11 Inn (5)
12 Highly confidential (3,6)
17 Marks as correct (5)
19 Parody (7)
21 Rich stew from Hungary (7)
22 Shin bone (5)
23 Soldier in the Royal Engineers (6)
24 Avaricious (6)

DOWN

1 Serious altercation (4-2)
2 Bolt hole (7)
3 Soft creamy sweet (5)
5 Gamekeeper's opponent (7)
6 Accounting entry showing sums owing (5)
7 Puzzle (6)
9 Covertly (2,7)
13 Corridor (7)
14 Strife (7)
15 Phases (6)
16 Anxious (6)
18 Fool (5)
20 Travel by car (5)

Solution see page 245

50

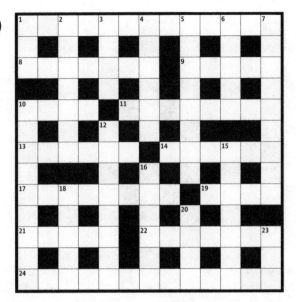

ACROSS

1 Policy of twofold security? (4,3,6)
8 Large cat (7)
9 Cost (5)
10 Friend (4)
11 London street with many private clubs (4,4)
13 Annoyed (6)
14 Member of the Beatles, d. 1980 (6)
17 Went beyond (8)
19 Characteristic features of behaviour (4)
21 Negotiate to reach an agreement (5)
22 Embellish unreasonably (4–3)
24 Confused (13)

DOWN

1 Large soft bread roll (3)
2 Listlessness (7)
3 Causing steady dull pain (4)
4 Cathedral city on the River Wear (6)
5 Caused to feel intense aversion (8)
6 Porcelain (5)
7 Archipelago off the north coast of Scotland (9)
10 Happy (9)
12 Device for monitoring hazards (8)
15 Most imminent (7)
16 Overthrow (6)
18 Board game (5)
20 Exploit (4)
23 Superhuman being (3)

Solution see page 245

51

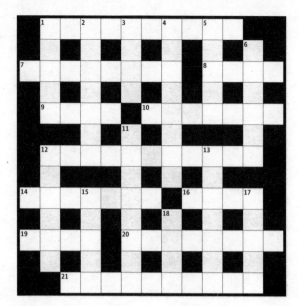

ACROSS

1 1948 Cole Porter musical (4,2,4)
7 Baked mixture of egg whites and sugar (8)
8 Court order (4)
9 Gentlewoman (4)
10 Science of animal life (7)
12 Solid figure with five plane faces (11)
14 Web access program (7)
16 Pound (slang) (4)
19 Feral — crazy (4)
20 Instruction (8)
21 Construction worker (10)

DOWN

1 Funereal bell sound (5)
2 Large Wiltshire railway town (7)
3 Gullible people (4)
4 Capsize (4,4)
5 Drying cloth (5)
6 Maiden (6)
11 Regal — grand (8)
12 Official document giving authorisation (6)
13 Approximately (7)
15 Broader (5)
17 Small US restaurant (5)
18 Toad ___ (Toad's home) (4)

Solution see page 245

52

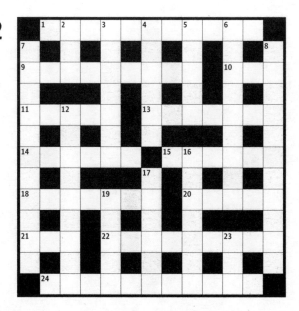

ACROSS

1 West Hollywood entertainment thoroughfare (6,5)

9 Not indulging appetite for food or drink (9)

10 Compete (3)

11 Rowed (5)

13 Circular floral head decoration (7)

14 Nickname of the Great Bell of the Palace of Westminster (3,3)

15 Maximum (6)

18 Divulge information about someone's secret or criminal activity (5,2)

20 Faithful (5)

21 Dec's long-time partner (3)

22 Field event — value plot (anag) (4,5)

24 Surface made with irregular pieces of stone (5,6)

DOWN

2 Increases (3)

3 Stick or pin used in spinning (7)

4 Ditch (6)

5 Private instructor (5)

6 List of items present (9)

7 Arm of the Atlantic bordering western Europe (3,2,6)

8 Participant in a competition involving seven track and field events (11)

12 Controlling device (9)

16 Israeli city (3,4)

17 Release from a restraint (6)

19 Yellow quartz used for gemstones (5)

23 Large pot for making tea (3)

Solution see page 245

53

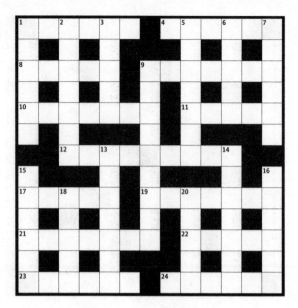

ACROSS

1 Hero of The Jungle Book (6)
4 One who avoids work (6)
8 Sleeper's vision (5)
9 Promised (7)
10 Relative by marriage (7)
11 French pancake (5)
12 Water-based paint (9)
17 Italian city noted for ham (5)
19 Synopsis — silhouette (7)
21 Give for safekeeping (7)
22 Momentary flash of light (5)
23 Feeling of despair in the face of obstacles (6)
24 Source (6)

DOWN

1 One of three sisters with snakes for hair (6)
2 Saturday and Sunday (7)
3 Buddhist monks (5)
5 Patella (7)
6 Hazy (5)
7 Ship's steering device (6)
9 Whit Sunday (9)
13 Broad-bladed kitchen implement (7)
14 Barrier — complaining bitterly (7)
15 Sustained (6)
16 Defeated (6)
18 Religious observances (5)
20 Striped quadruped (5)

Solution see page 246

54

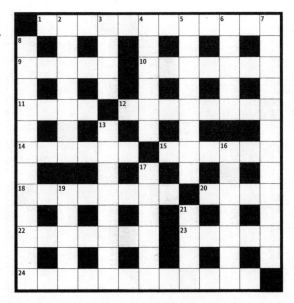

ACROSS

1 Flue cleaner (7,5)

9 U-shaped curve in a stream (5)

10 (Of climate) more pleasantly warm (7)

11 Adam and Eve's third son (4)

12 Thick slice of bread (8)

14 Up-to-date (4,2)

15 French-speaking Canadian provincial capital (6)

18 Water sport (8)

20 Flat circular plate (4)

22 Put right (4,3)

23 On your bike! (3,2)

24 Treatment aimed at recovering suppressed memories (12)

DOWN

2 Environment in which groups normally live (7)

3 Cut down with a blade (4)

4 All together (2,4)

5 Tanning salon (8)

6 Force out (5)

7 Astute intelligence (12)

8 Terminates (4,4,4)

13 Brilliant — prodigy (8)

16 1990s' style of UK music (7)

17 Telltale (6)

19 Munch noisily (5)

21 Soft swishing sound (4)

Solution see page 246

55

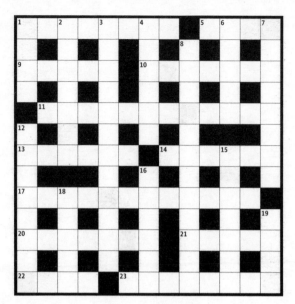

ACROSS

1 Practitioner (8)
5 Percussion instrument (4)
9 Nobleman (5)
10 Incite to action (7)
11 Eventually (2,3,4,3)
13 Messenger (6)
14 Sign of the zodiac (6)
17 Heartbroken (12)
20 Crimson (7)
21 Author of Adam Bede, d. 1880 (5)
22 Walk through water (4)
23 Used up (8)

DOWN

1 Flows back (4)
2 Associate (7)
3 With composure (12)
4 Incendiary liquid used in firebombs (6)
6 Scent (5)
7 Foliage (8)
8 In perfect condition — laudable sons (anag) (5,2,1,4)
12 Powered cutter (8)
15 String player (7)
16 Raid — short trip (6)
18 Beet with edible white leaf stalks (5)
19 Male horse kept for breeding (4)

Solution see page 246

56

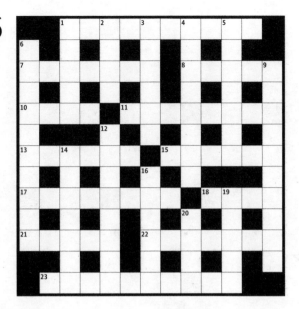

ACROSS

1 Trick (10)

7 Vent (7)

8 Repeat performance (5)

10 19th-century demon barber of Fleet Street (4)

11 Huge setback (4,4)

13 Internet filming device (6)

15 Large fleet (6)

17 Relating to the newborn (8)

18 Deer with antlers (4)

21 Cavalry sword (5)

22 Usual pattern of actions (7)

23 Shade of navy — talented university sportsperson (6,4)

DOWN

1 Horse (5)

2 Minor (and temporary) deviation from trend (4)

3 Milky winter punch (3-3)

4 Area surrounded by agricultural buildings (8)

5 Large chest-beating ape (7)

6 Quick nap (5,5)

9 Modern and familiar (10)

12 Capital of Bosnia-Herzegovina (8)

14 Ghetto blaster (4,3)

16 European capital (6)

19 Rubbish (edible, maybe) (5)

20 Cloudy — tedious (4)

Solution see page 246

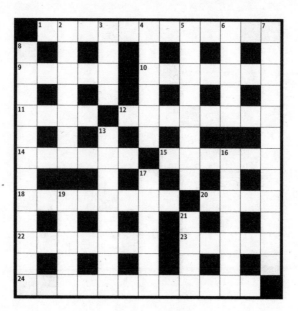

ACROSS

1 Musical talent (one appreciated by batsmen?) (7,5)
9 Excessive self-esteem (5)
10 Spirited — stylish (7)
11 Smell bad (4)
12 Leader of the Roundheads, d. 1658 (8)
14 Writer (6)
15 Not observed (6)
18 Completely sealed (8)
20 Coronation Street? (4)
22 Advantage (7)
23 Person born under the first sign of the zodiac (5)
24 Making one feel lively and cheerful (12)

DOWN

2 Distinguished (7)
3 Anguish (4)
4 Sacred (anag) — trees (6)
5 Shawl made of high quality goat's wool (8)
6 Group related by blood or marriage (5)
7 Small horse from Scotland (8,4)
8 Friendly (12)
13 Strong (8)
16 Agitation of mind (7)
17 More healthy — worker (6)
19 American stock farm (5)
21 Survive (4)

Solution see page 247

58

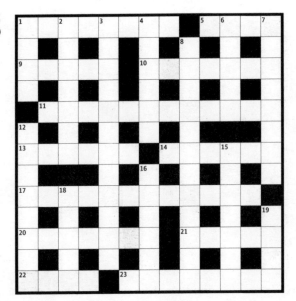

ACROSS

1 Warship smaller than a frigate (8)
5 Mineral used as a toiletry (4)
9 Turn out (5)
10 Swarming (with) (7)
11 Meanwhile (3,3,6)
13 Free and easy (6)
14 Elevation (6)
17 Completely normal (2,2,8)
20 Stream in north Italy that Julius Caesar crossed in 49 BC (7)
21 Arrive at (5)
22 Pitcher (4)
23 Windy (8)

DOWN

1 Sailors — boasted (4)
2 Destructive (7)
3 Business that sells and rents properties for clients (6,6)
4 Move unsteadily (6)
6 Get up (5)
7 Think deeply (8)
8 Be dismissed from one's employment (3,4,5)
12 Without penalty (4-4)
15 Small bomb (7)
16 Relating to the backbone (6)
18 Holy Scripture (5)
19 Watery part of milk (4)

Solution see page 247

59

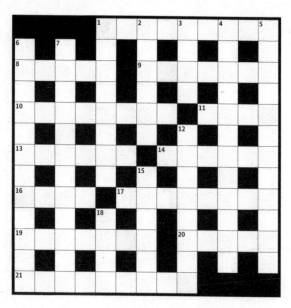

ACROSS

1 Moved from its proper position (9)
8 Spacious (5)
9 Means (7)
10 First concern (8)
11 Roman emperor, d. AD 68 (4)
13 Oscillate (6)
14 Moving crowd of people (6)
16 Leave the stage (4)
17 Mixed raw vegetables served as an hors d'oeuvre (8)
19 Sea eagles (7)
20 Canal boat (5)
21 Table napkin (9)

DOWN

1 Dawn (8)
2 Ill-tempered (informal) (6)
3 Previous (4)
4 Hothouse (12)
5 Having been deprived of property, land etc (12)
6 Utterly absurd (12)
7 Risque romantic historical novel (6,6)
12 Able to be ordered in quality, size etc (8)
15 Good health (6)
18 Beautiful fairy (4)

Solution see page 247

60

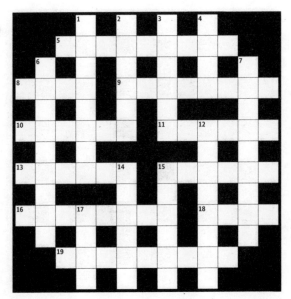

ACROSS

5 Byname — Boers quit (anag) (9)
8 Ceremonial elegance and splendour (4)
9 Short-distance attempt to reach the green (4,4)
10 Andean bird (6)
11 Stroke of bad luck (6)
13 Biographical film (6)
15 In high spirits (6)
16 Shame (8)
18 Abound (4)
19 Horse-drawn carriage with two seats and a folding hood (9)

DOWN

1 (Of an engine) made more powerful (6,2)
2 Restorative drink (6)
3 Wriggle with embarrassment (6)
4 Converted stables (4)
6 Sleep inducing (9)
7 Be missing (or stolen) (2,7)
12 More devious (8)
14 Seats (that can be electric or musical) (6)
15 Muscle that bends a joint (6)
17 Constellation — lecher (4)

Solution see page 247

61

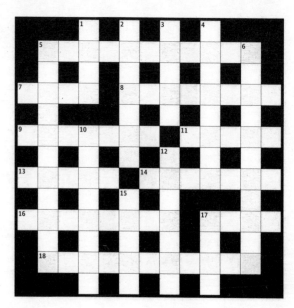

ACROSS

5 Decline and Fall author (6,5)
7 Bloke (4)
8 Bony part of neck of veal or mutton (5-3)
9 Scrap (of information, news etc) (7)
11 Writings not in verse (5)
13 Name of eight English kings (5)
14 State capital of Georgia (7)
16 Mild attack of epilepsy (French) (5,3)
17 Company emblem (4)
18 Conveyed — enraptured (11)

DOWN

1 Profound (4)
2 Travellers (7)
3 Fencer's weapon (5)
4 European country (8)
5 Quality improvement (11)
6 Genuine (6-2-3)
10 Enthusiastic supporter (8)
12 Strong English cheese, originally from Leicestershire (7)
15 Entertain (5)
17 Oodles (4)

Solution see page 248

62

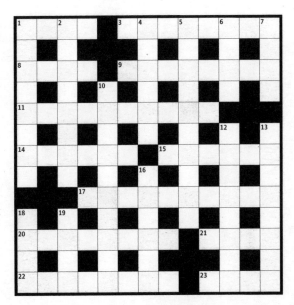

ACROSS

1 Inventor of the ballpoint (4)

3 Mad — hen dug in (anag) (8)

8 Youngsters (4)

9 Laws (8)

11 Entitled to high esteem (10)

14 Portuguese capital (6)

15 Spanish fleet sent in 1588 to escort an invasion of England (6)

17 Able to grasp an object — Helen is rep (anag) (10)

20 Dissertation (8)

21 Young deer (4)

22 At once (8)

23 Marine mammal (4)

DOWN

1 Place to escape from danger (8)

2 Discourtesy (8)

4 Acceptable (3,3)

5 Lacking respect for the beliefs of others (10)

6 Fortitude and determination (4)

7 Drug (4)

10 Totalitarian (10)

12 Fence consisting of stakes (8)

13 Motherly (8)

16 Hand tool (6)

18 Small rounded earring (4)

19 Mock (4)

Solution see page 248

63

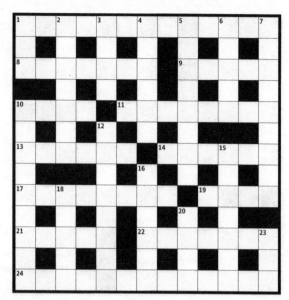

ACROSS

1 Top-level conference (6,7)
8 Audio file distributed over the internet (7)
9 German philosopher, d. 1831 (5)
10 Covering for the face (4)
11 On the other side of the page (8)
13 Change for the better (6)
14 Superhero, Robin's partner (6)
17 Presiding officer (8)
19 Small Scottish island (4)
21 Colourless gas, O_3 (5)
22 Kind of duck (7)
24 Fireproof device at the front of a theatre stage (6,7)

DOWN

1 Drain (3)
2 Diaphragm area (7)
3 Tablet computer from Apple (4)
4 Reason behind an action (6)
5 Of the spirit (8)
6 Fireplace (5)
7 Small bird with yellow and black wings (9)
10 Excessively greedy (9)
12 Salacious (8)
15 North-west US state bordering Canada (7)
16 Road surface (6)
18 Eichmann's given name (5)
20 Make less clear (4)
23 Put on (3)

Solution see page 248

64

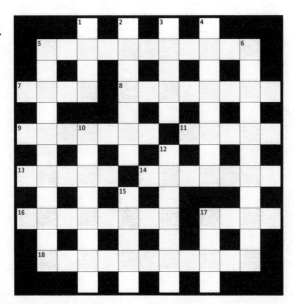

ACROSS

5 Proceed without advance planning (4,2,2,3)

7 Arduous journey (4)

8 Formal agreement between two or more parties (8)

9 Rebuked angrily (7)

11 Lukewarm (5)

13 Woman's scarf worn about the shoulders (5)

14 Scientific study of animals (7)

16 Close at hand (8)

17 Oaths (4)

18 Welsh textile and fashion designer, d. 1985 (5,6)

DOWN

1 Just a bit of fun (4)

2 Female dogs (7)

3 Over (5)

4 Want to he helpful (4,4)

5 Common analgesic (11)

6 Absconding (7,4)

10 Land visited by Gulliver (8)

12 Competition (7)

15 Gurkhas' homeland (5)

17 Detestable (4)

Solution see page 248

65

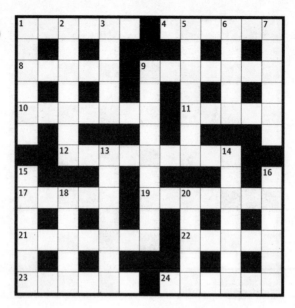

ACROSS

1 Very (4,2)
4 Little angel (6)
8 Weatherproof jacket (5)
9 Animated film (7)
10 Attacked (3,4)
11 Carmen, for example (5)
12 Capable (9)
17 Take (an exam) again (5)
19 Paper fasteners (7)
21 Absentees from school (7)
22 Backhander (5)
23 Evening meal (6)
24 Heavy — plodding (6)

DOWN

1 City on the Rio Grande (2,4)
2 Unpredictable (7)
3 Skin of the head (5)
5 Internal secretion — moorhen (anag) (7)
6 French wine region (5)
7 Author of The Pilgrim's Progress (6)
9 General agreement (9)
13 Daytime performance (7)
14 Corresponded (7)
15 Free of charge (6)
16 (Of a ship) behind (6)
18 Drink noisily (5)
20 Stroll (5)

Solution see page 249

66

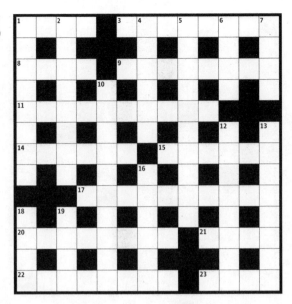

ACROSS

1 Dexterous (4)

3 Senior official of the House of Lords (5,3)

8 Have trust (in) (4)

9 Tries (8)

11 On the level (5,5)

14 Not dextrous (6)

15 Spread out untidily (6)

17 Hands-on medics (10)

20 Liqueur containing raw eggs (8)

21 Historic Scottish county, bordering on the Firth of Forth (4)

22 Genetic make-up (8)

23 Bombard — animal skin (4)

DOWN

1 State of temporary inaction (8)

2 Continuation (6-2)

4 Liquid preparation for the skin (6)

5 Selectively choose the best from what's available (6-4)

6 Of poor quality (4)

7 Sprint (4)

10 Marry (3,7)

12 Periodical publication (8)

13 Handbill — extra protection for a tent (8)

16 Unscathed (6)

18 Launder (4)

19 Declare positively (4)

Solution see page 249

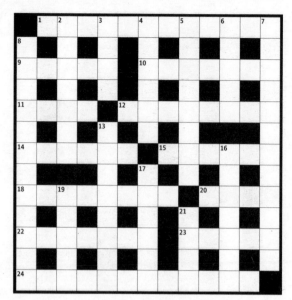

ACROSS

1 Cheesy dish (5,7)
9 Piercing (5)
10 Have faith (7)
11 Financial institution (4)
12 Blood feud (8)
14 Slackness (6)
15 Gulf port — sweet grape (6)
18 City straddling the Bosporus (8)
20 Stateside season (4)
22 Pickled herring (7)
23 Potential oak (5)
24 Church window material (7,5)

DOWN

2 When the sun crosses the equator (7)
3 Appear (4)
4 Red gems (6)
5 Excluded as a possibility (5,3)
6 Lamb's cry (5)
7 TS Eliot's long 1922 poem (3,5,4)
8 Pub game (3,9)
13 Movie extra who does the dangerous bits (8)
16 Soft leather (7)
17 Leapt (6)
19 Oklahoma city (5)
21 Follow — rear end (4)

68

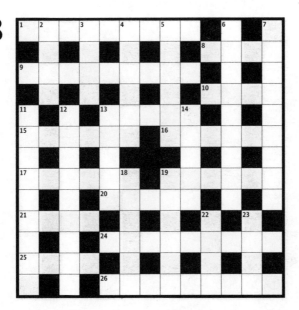

ACROSS

1,9 American author of the Tarzan stories, d. 1950 (5,4,9)
8 Bird — flying toy (4)
9 See 1
10 A small drink of liquor (4)
13 Caught — picked up (5)
15 Departs (6)
16 Uncontrolled anger (6)
17 Concurs (6)
19 Deep, narrow gorge (6)
20 Seedy nightclubs (5)
21 Large number (of ants?) (4)
24,26 Act quite inappropriately for the occasion (6,3,5,4)
25 Spots (4)
26 See 24

DOWN

2 Medication (4)
3 Wrong — twisted to one side (4)
4 Excites (6)
5 Group of those of approximately the same age — Roman military unit (6)
6 Episcopate (9)
7 Anxious (9)
11 Remove objects from the table after a meal (5,4)
12 Eucharist, for example (9)
13 Cut with blows (5)
14 French artist known for his ballet scenes, d. 1917 (5)
18 Artist's model (6)
19 Ignore (anag) — expanse of land (6)
22 Flowerless plant with feathery fronds (4)
23 Close (4)

Solution see page 249

69

ACROSS

1 German Romantic composer of orchestral and choral works, d. 1847 (11)
9 Underground worker (4,5)
10 Sound expressing disapproval (3)
11 Piece of cutlery (5)
13 Absorb (7)
14 Bureau (6)
15 Fine parchment (6)
18 Foul in rugby (5,2)
20 Gripping device with two hinged legs (5)
21 Dove-like noise (3)
22 Unpolished food grains (5,4)
24 Cause of much misery (11)

DOWN

2 Historical period (3)
3 As if possessed (7)
4 Theatrical knife (6)
5 Twig (5)
6 Sprite (9)
7 Footballer's bicycle attempt on goal (7,4)
8 Master of ceremonies at a banquet (11)
12 Out of sorts (3,6)
16 Out of existence (7)
17 Out of fashion (6)
19 Meat dish served on skewers (5)
23 Traditional affirmation to some marriage vows (1,2)

Solution see page 250

70

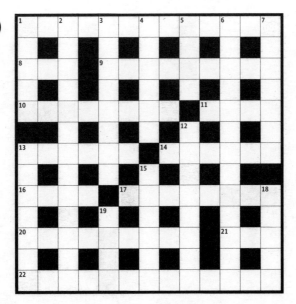

ACROSS

1 Series of small amounts (5,3,5)
8 Negation of what follows (3)
9 Confounded (9)
10 Ground almond paste (8)
11 Semi-solid mass — dunce (4)
13 Beer maker (6)
14 Forever (6)
16 Hazard (4)
17 Middle-of-the-road reflectors (4,4)
20 Beach vehicle with large tyres (4,5)
21 Lughole (3)
22 Forecast software problem for New Year's Day 2000 (10,3)

DOWN

1 Thick cotton cloth (5)
2 Relating to relationships (13)
3 Will do (8)
4 Nutty sweet (6)
5 Two nickels (4)
6 Be, do or have, for example, grammatically — I buy Rex a rival (anag) (9,4)
7 Calms (7)
12 Gesundheit! (5,3)
13 Monotony (7)
15 Journalese or legalese, say? (6)
18 Shoulder movement (5)
19 Skilled (4)

Solution see page 250

71

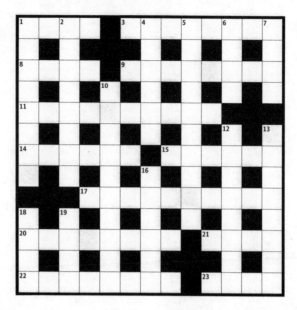

ACROSS

1 Vessel (for gravy?) (4)
3 Disciple (8)
8 Food (slang) (4)
9 Coffee-flavoured liqueur (3,5)
11 Lindisfarne (4,6)
14 Stringed instrument (6)
15 Star system (6)
17 Composer of the musical Oliver! (6,4)
20 Spectator (8)
21 The ___ of the Greasepaint — The Smell of the Crowd (1964 musical) (4)
22 Inflexibility (8)
23 Travel permit (4)

DOWN

1 Libya's second most populous city (8)
2 Not subject to any limitation (8)
4 Songbird with yellow and black plumage — Leo or I (anag) (6)
5 Pitiful (10)
6 Small hard excrescence on the skin (4)
7 Peruse(d) (4)
10 Probability (10)
12 Pasta tubes (8)
13 Uncontrollable emotion — this year (anag) (8)
16 Move away from the left margin (6)
18 Rain heavily (4)
19 Iris — become weary (4)

Solution see page 250

72

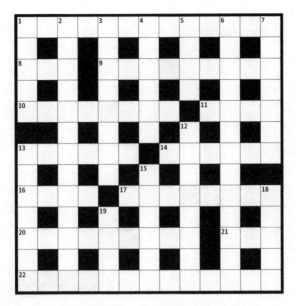

ACROSS

1 Calm and stoical in the face of setbacks (13)
8 Bark in quick sharp bursts (3)
9 Lack of confidence (4–5)
10 Examining with attention (8)
11 Asterisk (4)
13 Tripped the light fantastic (6)
14 Saunter (6)
16 Fringe benefit (4)
17 Yellowing of the skin and whites of the eyes (8)
20 Represented in simplified form (9)
21 Hawaiian garland of flowers (3)
22 Be the deciding factor (3,3,7)

DOWN

1 Discharge a debt (3,2)
2 Affiliated (2,11)
3 Showing compulsive interest (8)
4 Available via the internet (6)
5 Animal skin (4)
6 Stock made from vegetables and wine — botulin colour (anag) (5,8)
7 Avoiding embellishment (7)
12 Distinctive of group ways of living (8)
13 Down payment (7)
15 Of Cambridge University (6)
18 Pick of the bunch (5)
19 Chinese nursemaid (4)

Solution see page 250

73

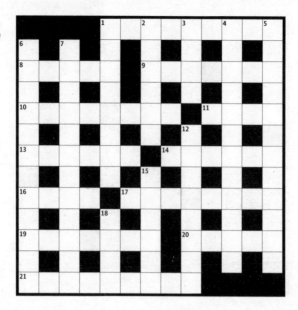

ACROSS

1 Easy target for a loan (4,5)
8 Totally exhausted (3,2)
9 Outburst of applause (7)
10 Increase rapidly (8)
11 Open wagon (to come after, not before, the horse) (4)
13 Attire worn by women riders (6)
14 Understanding (6)
16 Disease–causing bacterium (4)
17 Participate (4,4)
19 Court-ordered maintenance (7)
20 Put a price on (5)
21 Dinner she (anag) — held as sacred (9)

DOWN

1 Dotage (8)
2 Unfriendly (6)
3 Gin — hidden danger (4)
4 Impossible to conceive (12)
5 Produce a coherent whole (4,8)
6 Reach the desired standard (4,3,5)
7 Fruit (12)
12 Shy (8)
15 Deep gorge (6)
18 Coarse fibre from a coconut husk (4)

Solution see page 251

74

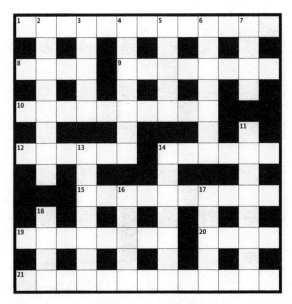

ACROSS

1 Too much to be reckoned (6,7)
8 Greek letter — second in order of importance (4)
9 Residential district on a city's outskirts (8)
10 In an intimate manner (10)
12 US president, 1929-33 (6)
14 Money-making scheme (6)
15 Beach fortification? (10)
19 Cornucopia — superfluity (8)
20 Implore (4)
21 Typical Mississippi vessel (6,7)

DOWN

2 Lifting device (8)
3 Animal of the giraffe family (much loved by crossword setters) (5)
4 File (7)
5 Still smouldering fragment of wood or coal (5)
6 Atomiser (7)
7 Maraud (4)
11 Fellow prisoner (8)
13 Called on (7)
14 Beguile (7)
16 Loop formed by means of a slip knot (5)
17 Brown pigment produced from cuttlefish ink (5)
18 Humble request for help (4)

Solution see page 251

75

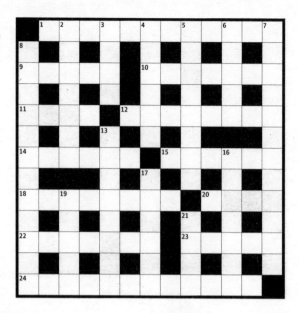

ACROSS

1 Just the very best (3,4,5)
9 Silly billy (5)
10 Employees' restaurant (7)
11 Cure (4)
12 Eastern (8)
14 Thoroughly soaked (6)
15 Leave a sailing vessel unable to move for lack of wind (6)
18 As opposed to digital (8)
20 City in Normandy (4)
22 Storm (7)
23 Make amends (5)
24 Tory creed (12)

DOWN

2 Official record of parliamentary debates (7)
3 Lads (4)
4 Accompany (6)
5 Author of One Flew Over the Cuckoo's Nest, d. 2001 (3,5)
6 DVD player button (5)
7 Very determined (6-6)
8 Gung-ho (12)
13 Suicide (Anglo-Latin) — dole fees (anag) (4,2,2)
16 Totally bewildered (2,1,4)
17 Holst or Mahler? (6)
19 Process of running an organisation (abbr) (5)
21 Way of walking (4)

Solution see page 251

76

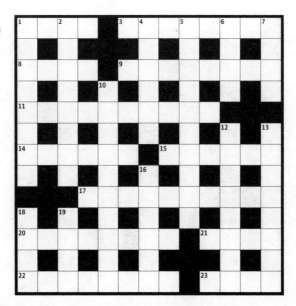

ACROSS

1 Cold-shoulder (4)

3 (Patronisingly) educational (8)

8 Sheep (4)

9 Remove one's clothes (5,3)

11 Contemptuous (10)

14 Finger-shaped cream-filled cake of choux pastry (6)

15 Place where everything is perfect (6)

17 Green or yellow liqueur made by monks (10)

20 Grill over an open fire (8)

21 State of mental agitation (4)

22 Look on (8)

23 Become threadbare (4)

DOWN

1 More stable (8)

2 With apprehension (8)

4 Mean (6)

5 Beekeeping (10)

6 Stole (4)

7 Tea shop (4)

10 Expatriation (10)

12 Articulate confusedly, as in a rage (8)

13 Die out (4,4)

16 French novelist — stupor (anag) (6)

18 Large wading bird (4)

19 Scottish hillside (4)

Solution see page 251

77

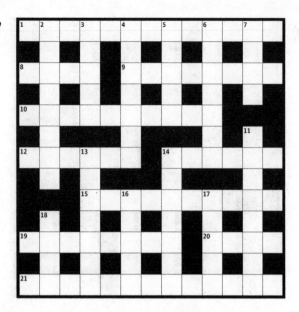

ACROSS

1 Port at the mouth of the Tees (13)
8 Surrounded by (4)
9 "Been there, ___" (4,4)
10 Agnes Grey author, d. 1849 (4,6)
12 Unidirectional (3-3)
14 Moon of Mars (6)
15 Extravagant (10)
19 Boxer (8)
20 1941 cinematic citizen (4)
21 eg "She sells seashells by the seashore" (6-7)

DOWN

2 About to happen (8)
3 Take evasive action (5)
4 Getting on (7)
5 French-speaking West African country (5)
6 Moving — active (2,3,2)
7 Clothes — paraphernalia (4)
11 Carry on (8)
13 North Atlantic food fish (7)
14 Cornish seaside resort (7)
16 Corn (5)
17 Garden tools (5)
18 Olympic combat sport (4)

Solution see page 252

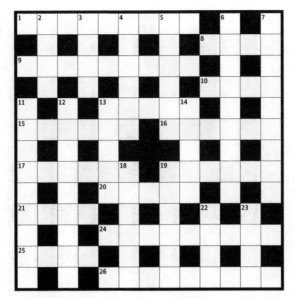

ACROSS

1 Retreat from a previously held position (9)
8 Mist (4)
9 Document included with a letter (9)
10 Strip off — Manx port (4)
13 Swoon (5)
15 Numbering more than one (6)
16 A butcher's — bird (6)
17 Gossip (6)
19 Caress — golf shot (6)
20 Rot (5)
21 Undercooked (4)
24 Having four feet (9)
25 Lot — doom (4)
26 Party with lots of food and drink (9)

DOWN

2 Wound dressing (4)
3 Spot — a spy (4)
4 Depressing (6)
5 Electrical circuitry (6)
6 Listen in (9)
7 Used before and reliable (4-5)
11 Fine snow driven by the wind (9)
12 Self-denial of pleasures (9)
13 Washed out (5)
14 Flavoursome (5)
18 Chide (6)
19 Make unhappy (6)
22 Contemplate — a goddess of the liberal arts (4)
23 Low-lying wetlands (4)

Solution see page 252

79

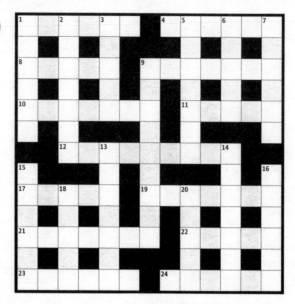

ACROSS

1 Device for controlling apparatus from a distance (6)
4 Place of worship with an altar (6)
8 Irish painter, d. 1992 (5)
9 Garden fertiliser (7)
10 Batsmen going in first (7)
11 In that place (5)
12 Sheltered (9)
17 Author of many fables (5)
19 Placate (7)
21 Tasty (7)
22 Completely — to some extent (5)
23 Guildford's county (6)
24 Heaviness (6)

DOWN

1 Start (a computer) again (6)
2 Shakespeare's Scottish play (7)
3 Not relaxed (5)
5 Rodent kept as a pet (7)
6 Demonstrate conclusively (5)
7 Missive (6)
9 Usual (9)
13 Ecstasy (7)
14 Pencilled picture (7)
15 Girls (6)
16 Vanquish (6)
18 Cut off (5)
20 Resentment at a slight (5)

Solution see page 252

80

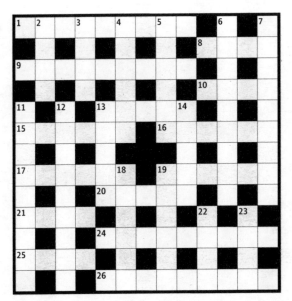

ACROSS

1 Tend towards (9)

8 Blocking vote (4)

9 Journey plan (9)

10 Miserable — cerulean (4)

13 Leader — line-drawing aid (5)

15 BBC — relative (6)

16 Fight between rival gangs of adolescents (6)

17 Antidepressant (6)

19 Night-time pest (6)

20 French river (5)

21 Adjust for better performance (4)

24 French Riviera (4,5)

25 A very long time (4)

26 Musicians playing oil drums (5,4)

DOWN

2 Speed — value (4)

3 Fin attached to the tail of an arrow (4)

4 Force causing rotation (6)

5 Artist — wheel? (6)

6 (Infant?) sweet (5,4)

7 13 across — coin (9)

11 Presumptuously seek success in a new locality — eg tap crab (anag) (9)

12 Radio or television reader (9)

13 Someone you hope to defeat (5)

14 Indian coin (5)

18 Failure to face some difficulty squarely (3-3)

19 Light wind (6)

22 Coat with plaster (4)

23 Incinerate (4)

Solution see page 252

81

ACROSS

1 Capital of North Rhine–Westphalia (10)

7 Cage holding poultry (7)

8 Place of calm in troubled times (5)

10 Spanish currency (4)

11 Parrot native to Australia and Indonesia (8)

13 Quell (6)

15 Make a piercing sound (6)

17 Sign of the zodiac (8)

18 Mop (4)

21 Danish currency (5)

22 Bewitching (7)

23 Social club for American male undergraduates (10)

DOWN

1 Organ giver? (5)

2 Black chimney powder (4)

3 Hire (6)

4 One method of scoring three points in rugby union (4,4)

5 Badge with a ribbon (7)

6 PS He has Ken (anag) — rope-shortening knot (10)

9 Tracked vehicle for winter travel? (10)

12 Nourishing substance (8)

14 Bedroom fit for a lady (7)

16 Warm season (6)

19 Bonkers (5)

20 Trademarked hybrid citrus fruit (4)

Solution see page 253

82

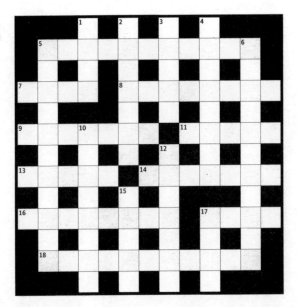

ACROSS

5 As knickers may be (11)

7 Rock music — American thug (4)

8 One of the original 13 colonies that formed the United States (8)

9 Gear (7)

11 Apron (abbr) (5)

13 Chasm (5)

14 Silliness (7)

16 Is it real? (anag) — kind of food poisoning (8)

17 Product of three equal numbers (4)

18 Portable communications device (6,5)

DOWN

1 Tree trunk's outer layer (4)

2 Perplexed — way to get out in cricket (7)

3 Neck warmer (5)

4 Male steed (8)

5 State of balance (11)

6 At which one eats — lending a bit (anag) (6,5)

10 Lab vessel (4,4)

12 Infelicitous (7)

15 Marxism's member of the working class (abbr) (5)

17 Yield — trim (4)

Solution see page 253

83

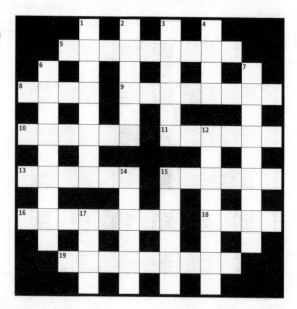

ACROSS

5 Vicar's neckwear (3,6)
8 A god to the French (4)
9 Uzbekistan capital (8)
10 Finicky (6)
11 Drink alcohol (6)
13 Fasten with short U-shaped bits of wire (6)
15 Stopped briefly (6)
16 Not guilty (8)
18 Temporary stitch (4)
19 Boisterous comedy (9)

DOWN

1 Television programme based on reality (8)
2 Feather-brained (6)
3 Small room (6)
4 One in favour of tough action (4)
6 Resist (9)
7 Sway (9)
12 Dressing to reduce inflammation (8)
14 Not liable (6)
15 Small and dainty (6)
17 Paris airport (4)

Solution see page 253

84

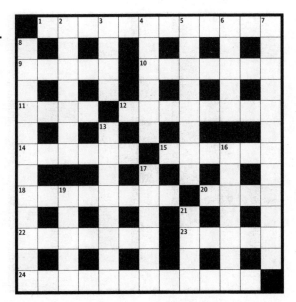

ACROSS

1 Irresistible — huge (12)

9 Device producing an intense beam of light or radiation (5)

10 New York port on the St Lawrence Seaway (7)

11 Musical symbol indicating pitch (4)

12 Ornamental design made of wood or metal strips (8)

14 Film on teeth that encourages caries (6)

15 Strong, well-built woman (6)

18 Dictatorial (8)

20 Silly little mistake (4)

22 Very silly (7)

23 Clamour (5)

24 Upsettingly emotional (3-9)

DOWN

2 Entrails — CIS rave (anag) (7)

3 Seldom seen (4)

4 Australian state capital (6)

5 Duration of existence (8)

6 Adult insect (5)

7 Percussion instrument — eg pink cellos (anag) (12)

8 Blood sausage (5,7)

13 Chunnel service (8)

16 Huge figure (7)

17 Baked beans container? (3,3)

19 Prescribed share of work (5)

21 Small Scottish island (4)

Solution see page 253

85

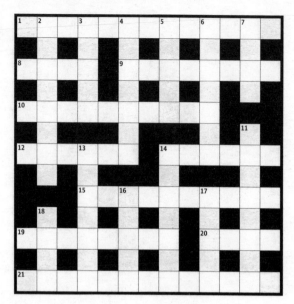

ACROSS

1 Children's party game (5,4,4)
8 Scheduled time — aperture for coins (4)
9 Short fluted tubes of pasta (8)
10 Small secondary flat or house (4-1-5)
12 Derided (6)
14 Threaten (6)
15 London rugby venue (10)
19 Exaggerated masculinity (8)
20 Dress (4)
21 British heir apparent (6,2,5)

DOWN

2 Sweet on a stick (8)
3 Observed (5)
4 Deserved (7)
5 African country dominated by the Sahara, until 1969 a French colony (5)
6 Booming bird (7)
7 Affectionate — tender (4)
11 Clambers (anag) — clamber (8)
13 Cook's place (7)
14 Leave hurriedly (4,3)
16 Offspring (5)
17 Roman (anag) — opera (5)
18 Two of a kind (4)

Solution see page 254

86

ACROSS

1 Died peacefully (7,4)

9 Hard, spicy beef and pork sausage (9)

10 Airtight metal container (3)

11 Repulsive (5)

13 Coming from the birthplace of Christopher Columbus (7)

14 Humorous play (6)

15 Mark Twain's character, Tom (6)

18 Civilians trained as soldiers (7)

20 Sheet (anag) — pronoun (5)

21 Bolt's partner (3)

22 Never-ending (9)

24 Again and again (11)

DOWN

2 Insolence (slang) (3)

3 Very drunk (3-4)

4 Plenty (6)

5 Arrange so as to be parallel (5)

6 Original model (9)

7 Promising (2-3-6)

8 Sweet nothings (11)

12 Fool (9)

16 Sinatra (anag) — skilled manual worker (7)

17 Group with shared concerns within a political party (6)

19 Strong thread (5)

23 Pointed tool for making small holes (3)

Solution see page 254

87

ACROSS

1 Up to the minute (6)
4 Aspect (5)
7 Turkish capital (6)
8 Jagged mountain range (6)
9 Wind instrument (4)
10 Recoil — bung (8)
12 Maker of circular wooden objects (11)
17 Rubber–bladed wiper for removing water (8)
19 Tip — top (4)
20 Philosopher's stone (6)
21 Camera stand (6)
22 Contaminate (5)
23 Cross (6)

DOWN

1 Powerful wooden weapon used against the French at Agincourt (7)
2 Flying circus apparatus? (7)
3 Electrical device fitted in the cylinder heads of an internal combustion engine (5,4)
4 Quick, light movement (5)
5 Place to get a vehicle clean (3,4)
6 Word of appreciation (6)
11 Woodwork (9)
13 Escape artist, Harry (7)
14 Person who cuts flat glass to size (7)
15 Small position from which future progress might be made (7)
16 Approval (6)
18 Legally binding order (5)

Solution see page 254

88

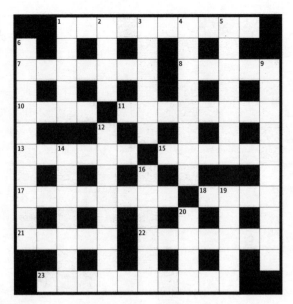

ACROSS

1 Board game for two players (10)
7 Angry dispute (7)
8 Friends (5)
10 Last word in prayer? (4)
11 Cloudburst (8)
13 Tank for heating water (6)
15 Member of the Religious Society of Friends (6)
17 Told (8)
18 Gratuities (4)
21 Protect (5)
22 Scoundrel (7)
23 Appropriate for the time of year (10)

DOWN

1 Teeth straightener (5)
2 Fish — find fault (4)
3 Imperial measure of capacity (6)
4 Impetus (8)
5 Prospect (7)
6 Bickering (10)
9 Astonishing (10)
12 Islands off north-west Scotland (8)
14 Blow up (7)
16 Paradise (6)
19 Incensed (5)
20 Smooth-talking (4)

Solution see page 254

89

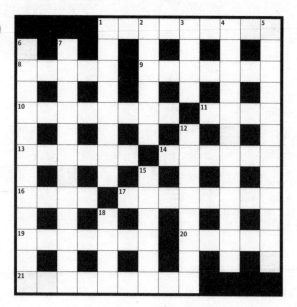

ACROSS

1 Those in second place (7-2)
8 High-pitched pig noises (5)
9 Theatrical knife? (7)
10 Peered-through aperture (8)
11 Filth (4)
13 Alliance — old measure of distance (6)
14 Scurry — frame worn under skirt (6)
16 Northern black and white diving birds (4)
17 Work out in a gym (4,4)
19 Archangel and messenger of God (7)
20 Deride — guzzle (5)
21 Voted back into office (2-7)

DOWN

1 When most people are going to or coming from work (4,4)
2 Settle cosily (6)
3 Isaac's eldest son (4)
4 Realm of A-list celebrity? (12)
5 Artist's spatula for mixing paints (7,5)
6 Ghostly double of a living person — green Lapp god (anag) (12)
7 Not particularly surprising (12)
12 Hypothetical (8)
15 Projectile (6)
18 Conflagration (4)

Solution see page 255

90

ACROSS

1 Indonesian holiday destination (4)
3 Strong, fit and active (8)
9 Nag (7)
10 Defraud (5)
11 Enticed (5)
12 Real (6)
14 Diverting activity (13)
17 Reveal the true nature of (6)
19 Ancient unit of length (5)
22 Transparent (5)
23 Nonsense (7)
24 Crushed by grief (8)
25 Profound — engrossed (4)

DOWN

1 Owing thanks (to) (8)
2 Recluse (5)
4 Become less important (4,1,4,4)
5 Allowable (5)
6 Adolescent (7)
7 Reductions (4)
8 Tributary (6)
13 Incriminate by unfair means (6,2)
15 £10 notes (7)
16 Stolen — arrested (6)
18 Month that's autumnal in Oz (5)
20 Hold responsible (5)
21 Corrosive liquid (4)

Solution see page 255

91

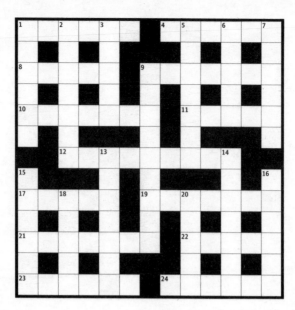

ACROSS

1 Coldish (6)

4 Throws (6)

8 Unwind (5)

9 High chest of drawers (7)

10 Tympanum (7)

11 With everything included (3–2)

12 Kind of recession where a brief recovery is followed by a further fall (6–3)

17 Long-distance walker (5)

19 Self-contradictory statement (7)

21 Amazing event (7)

22 Hard kind of stone — Welsh town on the Dee estuary (5)

23 Minutes played in a football match (6)

24 Joining of businesses (6)

DOWN

1 Firms operating together, illegally (6)

2 Badly brought up (3–4)

3 Egyptian city on the east bank of the Nile (5)

5 The Netherlands (7)

6 Conspiring group (5)

7 Maxim (6)

9 Kind of cinematic technique for showing a slow process at an accelerated pace (4–5)

13 Dutch city where peace treaties were signed to end the 1701–14 War of the Spanish Succession (7)

14 Sweet (7)

15 Medicine man (6)

16 South-west English city (6)

18 Holy book of Islam (5)

20 Gun with a long barrel (5)

Solution see page 255

ACROSS

1 Meddle (6)
4 Give money to (5)
7 Fanatic (6)
8 Sign of a learner driver (1–5)
9 Demolish (a building) (4)
10 Well-off (8)
12 Reduced the intensity of conflict (2–9)
17 Spreads through (8)
19 Son of Isaac and Rebecca (4)
20 Confesses (4,2)
21 Destructive swarming insect (6)
22 Happen afterwards as a result (5)
23 Provide evidence for (6)

DOWN

1 Shakespeare (3,4)
2 Someone from Valletta? (7)
3 Captivated (9)
4 Eject (5)
5 Crack shot (7)
6 Ring of flowers (6)
11 Fails to achieve the desired effect (5,4)
13 Small jobs (7)
14 Molasses (7)
15 Resolute — sedated (anag) (4,3)
16 Fight against (6)
18 Sky blue (5)

Solution see page 255

93

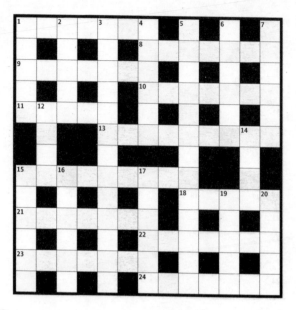

ACROSS

1 Branch of language study (7)
8 Artist's workroom (7)
9 Skipped (7)
10 Chanted (7)
11 Mortar missile (5)
13 Written or spoken communication (9)
15 Broken into bits (9)
18 Scarcely sufficient (5)
21 Funny (7)
22 With quickness and lightness (7)
23 Set piece of play in rugby (4-3)
24 Made changes to (7)

DOWN

1 Sheen (5)
2 Actor's remark for the audience alone (5)
3 Treasure hunter's tool (5,8)
4 Human forearm bone (6)
5 Watford's county (13)
6 Victor (6)
7 Game for four players (6)
12 WH Auden's middle name (4)
14 Observed (4)
15 Tool for cutting grain (6)
16 Edible nut (6)
17 Have to do with (6)
19 In the lead (5)
20 Engaged in an activity, but not seriously (5)

Solution see page 256

94

ACROSS

1 Something wished for (4)
3 Worthy of worship (8)
9 Ghost (7)
10 One of twelve in a box? (5)
11 Domesticated pack animal of the Andes (5)
12 Queen (6)
14 Parliamentary debate to approve the principles of a new bill — DNA recognised (anag) (6,7)
17 Counting machine (6)
19 Longest human bone (5)
22 Able to think clearly (5)
23 Tallest extant quadruped (7)
24 Nose hair pullers? (8)
25 Grape plant (4)

DOWN

1 Pocketed spirits container (3,5)
2 Shopping centre (5)
4 Light brown sweetener, originally from Guyana (8,5)
5 Put into a new order (5)
6 African country, on the shores of Lake Tanganyika, capital Bujumbura (7)
7 Book of the Old Testament (4)
8 Difficulty that causes tension (6)
13 Cause to feel sorrow (8)
15 Small room for special use (7)
16 Have the money for (6)
18 Old port of south-west Spain (5)
20 Civilian clothes for soldiers (5)
21 Even — pitched too low (4)

Solution see page 256

95

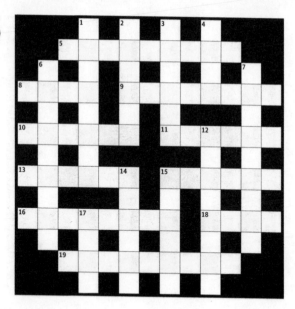

ACROSS

5 Building beside a railway track (6,3)
8 Floating platform (4)
9 Overdrawn (2,3,3)
10 Fracas (6)
11 Highly decorated (6)
13 Sharp bend (6)
15 Mark Antony's countrymen? (6)
16 Deep (8)
18 Virologist who developed a vaccine against polio, d. 1995 (4)
19 New Zealand rugby team (3,6)

DOWN

1 Relating to a shore (8)
2 Messy (6)
3 Helplessly drunk (6)
4 Fleshy part of the ear (4)
6 Dinner, bed and breakfast (4,5)
7 Four-sided figure (9)
12 Seek a man (anag) — one with an intimate connection? (8)
14 Dirty (6)
15 Type of tyre (6)
17 People (4)

Solution see page 256

96

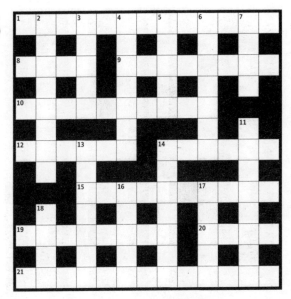

ACROSS

1 Musical based on a Hugo novel (3,10)

8 Skewer — exact likeness (4)

9 Self-defence method without weapons (8)

10 Someone learning to paint (3,7)

12 Hard worker (6)

14 Earl of Greystoke (6)

15 Magic drink stimulating desire (4,6)

19 Fire up again (8)

20 Ill-mannered (4)

21 Measure of weight in relation to height (4,4,5)

DOWN

2 Tsars (8)

3 Subject involving figures (abbr) (5)

4 Stay for a while (7)

5 Cosmetic powder (5)

6 Bubble on the skin filled with fluid (7)

7 Not hard (4)

11 Hug and kiss (8)

13 Merriment (7)

14 With chest totally exposed (7)

16 Russian spirit (5)

17 Italian city (with a shroud) (5)

18 Nil (4)

Solution see page 256

97

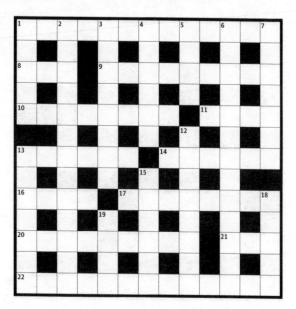

ACROSS

1 Delight in the troubles of others (13)

8 Apply friction to (3)

9 Overwhelming electoral victory (9)

10 Illustrative printed designs (8)

11 Powdery starch from a palm (4)

13 Region of France, once annexed by Prussia (6)

14 Manly (6)

16 Reverberate (4)

17 Quarter of a circle (8)

20 Female personification of Britain (9)

21 Freezing (3)

22 Somerset dairy product (7,6)

DOWN

1 Plant fibre used as fodder (5)

2 Option of taking what's on offer or getting nothing at all (7,6)

3 Tasty titbit (8)

4 Number of degrees in a right angle (6)

5 Got up (4)

6 Lacking any creativity (13)

7 Blight (7)

12 Ornamental outdoor basin — bad birth (anag) (4,4)

13 Bitter in taste — harsh in tone (7)

15 Private in the Royal Artillery (6)

18 Culinary herb of the mint family (5)

19 Shakespeare? (4)

Solution see page 257

98

ACROSS

1 Trek (4)
3 Gets into a snug position (8)
9 Meditate — throw back (7)
10 North-east Indian tea state (5)
11 Living organism, such as a shrub (5)
12 Piece of table linen (6)
14 Old Spanish coins (6,2,5)
17 College treasurer (6)
19 Alcoholic drink (5)
22 Spirit of Russia (5)
23 (Of a river) very fast flowing (2,5)
24 Vikings (8)
25 Catches in the act (4)

DOWN

1 Lively old sailors' dance (8)
2 Czech author of The Trial, d. 1924 (5)
4 Under no circumstances (3,2,4,4)
5 Lay hold of (5)
6 Permanent (7)
7 Reservoir for oil etc (4)
8 Kitchen utensil (6)
13 Competitors entered for a race (8)
15 South American country (7)
16 Forgive (6)
18 Frighten (5)
20 Roman goddess of the hunt (5)
21 River flowing into the Severn (4)

Solution see page 257

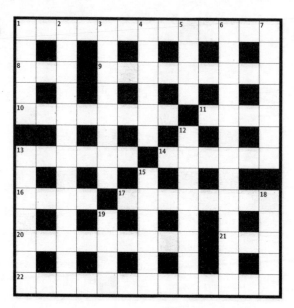

ACROSS

1 Police department dealing with political security (7,6)

8 Exploit (3)

9 Phone function using stored numbers (5,4)

10 Mechanism that switches something on — autocrat (anag) (8)

11 Fish related to the herring (4)

13 Change over (6)

14 Recollection (6)

16 Predatory black and white toothed whale (4)

17 French city with a cathedral renowned for its stained glass windows (8)

20 Put into an equilibrium (9)

21 Egg cells (3)

22 Pancake day (6,7)

DOWN

1 Aqualung (5)

2 Death row destination? (8,5)

3 Example (8)

4 Go to ground (3,3)

5 Batons (4)

6 Locality (13)

7 Vacation (7)

12 Behind (French) (8)

13 Husbands and wives (7)

15 Penny-pinching (6)

18 Frightening (5)

19 Ukraine's largest city (4)

100

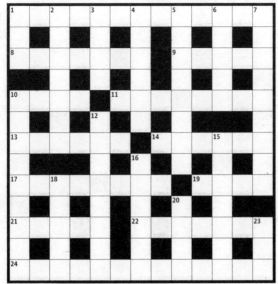

ACROSS

1 One whose political allegiance might easily change (8,5)

8 Imagine (5,2)

9 Balderdash (5)

10 Berkshire village with a 16th century vicar celebrated in legend and song (4)

11 Wrongdoer (8)

13 Double-breasted jacket for a man (6)

14 Tooth coating (6)

17 Cod catcher? (4,4)

19 Land in water (4)

21 Freshwater carnivorous mammal (5)

22 Stipulation (7)

24 Cheap melodramatic novel (5,8)

DOWN

1 Given sustenance (3)

2 Run (7)

3 Docile (4)

4 Tablecloths etc (6)

5 Violent (8)

6 North (anag) — point (5)

7 Queen's shade? (5,4)

10 Cake in a dish? (3,2,4)

12 Sloth (8)

15 Large short-haired dog breed (7)

16 Metal — officer (6)

18 Shiny fabric (5)

20 Fizzy drink (4)

23 Hooting bird (3)

Solution see page 257

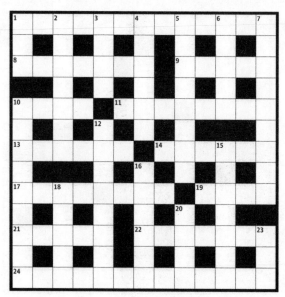

ACROSS

1 Renewal of cordial relations (13)
8 Central area of a city (7)
9 Mischievous trick (5)
10 Significant amount (1,3)
11 Neighbouring (8)
13 Making bread, cakes etc (6)
14 Supple (6)
17 16th-century French satirist, noted for earthy humour (8)
19 Dances — beer ingredient (4)
21 Lacerations (before bedtime?) (5)
22 Smiling broadly (7)
24 Total change in character (13)

DOWN

1 Droll (3)
2 Where horses are paraded before a race (7)
3 One is angry when one hits it (4)
4 Second largest country in the world by area (6)
5 Forceful in expression (8)
6 Exhilarate (5)
7 Alternate (4,5)
10 Garden where trees and shrubs are cultivated (9)
12 US government personification (5,3)
15 Turf accountants (7)
16 Feller's warning cry (6)
18 Explosion (5)
20 Goldberg Variations composer, d. 1750 (4)
23 Domestic fuel (3)

102

ACROSS

1 Work — party (6)
4 Burrowing desert rodent (6)
8 Dance — unexpected turn (5)
9 Transmission (7)
10 Began to wake (7)
11 Set of exam questions (5)
12 Sky (9)
17 Of a number system with base eight (5)
19 Use economically — partner (7)
21 Train with berths (7)
22 (Pop group) not affiliated with a major record company (5)
23 Harry, Dennis or Beatrix? (6)
24 Free-flowing (6)

DOWN

1 Most recent (6)
2 Sheriff's officer — landlord's agent (7)
3 Absolute — speak (5)
5 Model (7)
6 Form of modern jazz from about 1940 (5)
7 Opulence (6)
9 Mafia boss (9)
13 Fall back (7)
14 Stuff and nonsense (7)
15 Tittle-tattle (6)
16 Commercial (abbr) (6)
18 River that joins the Ouse to form the Humber (5)
20 Not moving (5)

Solution see page 258

103

ACROSS

5 Verbal abuse (4-7)
7 Saliva (4)
8 Hinged floor opening (8)
9 Small savoury snacks (7)
11 Circular (5)
13 Not silently (5)
14 Cambridge college founded by Henry VIII (7)
16 Reverie (8)
17 Tool with tines (4)
18 Jumping-off point (11)

DOWN

1 Flake of soot (4)
2 Strew (7)
3 Transparent (5)
4 Relax after stress (4,4)
5 A psalms unit (anag) — part of a Roman Catholic wedding (7,4)
6 Kind, friendly and patient (4-7)
10 Rocks (8)
12 Lincolnshire port (7)
15 French river — type of fishing net (5)
17 Young horse (4)

Solution see page 258

104

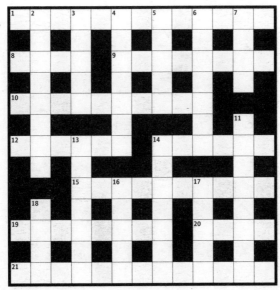

ACROSS

1 Out of favour (2,3,8)
8 Europe's highest active volcano (4)
9 Sexual purity (8)
10 Stare superstitiously believed to cause harm (3,4,3)
12 Convulsions (6)
14 Biblical book — group escape from a hostile environment (6)
15 Court game (4,6)
19 Compelling (8)
20 Trickle — weakling (4)
21 Compassionate (6-7)

DOWN

2 No chance at all! (3,1,4)
3 Drag (5)
4 Starched white shirt fronts (7)
5 Solemn — burial place (5)
6 Very busy (2,3,2)
7 Drunks (4)
11 Runaway (8)
13 Wed (7)
14 Immoderate (7)
16 Composer of Der Freischütz, d. 1826 (5)
17 All-time low (5)
18 Burden (4)

Solution see page 258

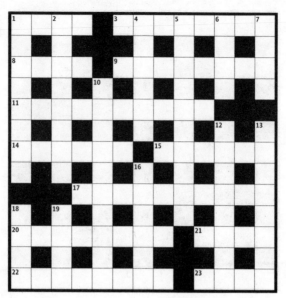

ACROSS

1 Theatre production (4)
3 Suddenly develop (6,2)
8 Pay a visit (4)
9 Climbing plant with colourful flowers (8)
11 Brotherhood (10)
14 Mediterranean island (6)
15 Norfolk seaside resort (6)
17 Disagreeable (10)
20 (Of medical procedures) not essential (8)
21 Attraction (4)
22 Heart-rending (8)
23 Salacious (4)

DOWN

1 One opposed to war (8)
2 Federation (8)
4 European country (6)
5 Irrelevant (10)
6 Pluck — intestines (4)
7 Energy (4)
10 Victor at Waterloo (10)
12 Not fully developed (8)
13 Wittered on (8)
16 Split (like some hoofs) (6)
18 Military vehicle (4)
19 Type of house (UK) — type of truck (US) (4)

Solution see page 259

106

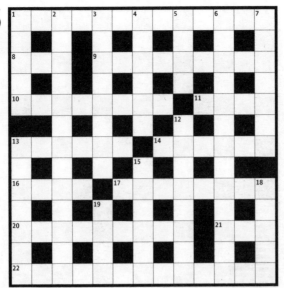

ACROSS

1 Australian ranch (6,7)

8 Lepidopterous floater, apian stinger, d. 2016 (3)

9 Domesticated cavy (6,3)

10 Liquid mixture of two or more substances (8)

11 Stop (4)

13 Central American country (6)

14 Passed through a sieve (6)

16 Portent (4)

17 Disadvantage (8)

20 Author of Go Set a Watchman, d. 2016 — paler here (anag) (6,3)

21 Form of jazz from the 1940s (3)

22 Type of butterfly (13)

DOWN

1 Category (5)

2 Empirical procedure (5,3,5)

3 Part of a wicket (3,5)

4 Former name of Ho Chi Minh City (6)

5 Caricatured (4)

6 Not feasible (13)

7 Nullified (7)

12 Old King Cole's trio (8)

13 Prognosticator (7)

15 Trees providing syrup (6)

18 Learner (5)

19 Captain of the Nautilus (4)

Solution see page 259

ACROSS

5 Seek to ingratiate oneself (5,6)
7 Twist out of shape (4)
8 Cocktail served in a tall glass (8)
9 City on the Clyde (7)
11 Attach (5)
13 Librettist Hammerstein, d. 1960 (5)
14 Story in three parts (7)
16 No old hat (anag) — chisel, for example (4,4)
17 Ladder part (4)
18 0 or 1 (6,5)

DOWN

1 Excursion (4)
2 Tropical cyclone (7)
3 Measuring device (5)
4 Unsure (8)
5 Author of Essays of Elia, d. 1834 (7,4)
6 Wealthy (7,2,2)
10 Social reputation (8)
12 Overture (7)
15 Woo (5)
17 Fury (4)

Solution see page 259

108

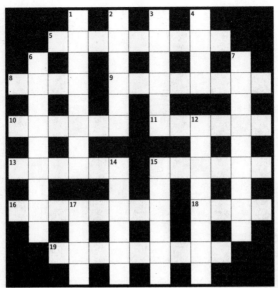

ACROSS

5 Relating to groups of atoms bonded together (9)

8 Anxiety (4)

9 Plant also called speedwell — I've no car (anag) (8)

10 Pants (6)

11 Change into a variant form (6)

13 Gems — Mick Jagger's rollers? (6)

15 One watching one's weight (6)

16 Lose emotional control (5,3)

18 Very top (4)

19 Vehicle thief (9)

DOWN

1 Pounds in a stone? (8)

2 Uneasy psychological state (6)

3 Minimum required number of members present for conducting business (6)

4 Type of thin linen or cotton (4)

6 Land (9)

7 Broadcast (9)

12 Youngster (8)

14 Capital of Macedonia (6)

15 Come off (6)

17 Unfortunately (4)

Solution see page 259

109

ACROSS

1 Astoundingly huge (10)
7 Hairdressers (8)
8 Go wrong (4)
9 Counterfeit (4)
10 Glazed biscuit shape of a loose knot (7)
12 Exploit (11)
14 Become popular (5,2)
16 Moolah (slang) (4)
19 Forbid outright (4)
20 Drink to whet the appetite (8)
21 As things turned out (2,3,5)

DOWN

1 Satisfies — asset (anag) (5)
2 Let go (7)
3 As an alternative (4)
4 Renegade (8)
5 Out of shape (5)
6 Take in (6)
11 War memorial (8)
12 Eased (6)
13 Arousing intense feeling (7)
15 Sing like Bing (5)
17 Lifting tackle (5)
18 Narrow wooded valley (4)

Solution see page 260

110

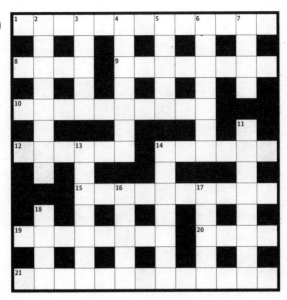

ACROSS

1 Item of seasonal soft sweet food (9,4)

8 Catch — problem (4)

9 Shorten (8)

10 Where kids can stroke and feed docile animals (7,3)

12 Musical composition with three or more contrasting movements (6)

14 Black and white striped animal (6)

15 Spirit said to leave money at night in compensation for losing a gnasher (5,5)

19 Consideration for others first (8)

20 Hop kiln (4)

21 Beyond description (13)

DOWN

2 Dependant (6-2)

3 Block of metal (5)

4 Fairy queen (7)

5 Excited (like a hive?) (5)

6 Man whose wife is cheating on him? (7)

7 Friends and acquaintances (4)

11 Counterattack (8)

13 Infectious sheep disease (7)

14 Nassau's island country (7)

16 Willow (5)

17 Garlic mayo (5)

18 Narrow mountain valley (4)

Solution see page 260

111

ACROSS

1 Dash (like a mouse?) (6)
4 Large jug (6)
8 Naomi (anag) — from Muscat? (5)
9 Grazing land (7)
10 Small field for horses (7)
11 Championship — form of address (5)
12 Extremely wicked (9)
17 Young eel (5)
19 To be won or lost (2,5)
21 Sweetening agent — Croesus (anag) (7)
22 Extra bit (3-2)
23 Musical line (6)
24 Eric Arthur Blair (6)

DOWN

1 Charlie Brown's canine companion (6)
2 From Kampala or Entebbe? (7)
3 Charging animal (5)
5 Country of southern Africa (7)
6 Haggard (5)
7 Necessary (6)
9 Card player's deadpan expression (5,4)
13 Permanently (3,4)
14 Wrap up (7)
15 Things thrown overboard and washed up ashore (6)
16 Strong-scented plant whose seeds and leaves are used in cookery (6)
18 Expressing opinions freely (5)
20 Flight unit? (5)

Solution see page 260

112

ACROSS

1 Rudimentary (9)
8 Grade (4)
9 Something of little value (9)
10 Fake (4)
13 To a superlative extent (2,3)
15 Men, women and children (6)
16 Turn back (6)
17 Amateur (6)
19 Gather into wrinkles (6)
20 Credit (5)
21 Hurt (4)
24 Volatile situation (9)
25 Insincere talk — slope (4)
26 Exaggeration for effect (9)

DOWN

2 Ramble without purpose (4)
3 Complain (4)
4 Colour knotted fabrics with swirling patterns (3-3)
5 Indecent (6)
6 Boisterousness (4,5)
7 Camel (9)
11 Washing machine or toaster, say (9)
12 Lightweight thermoplastic (9)
13 Cold and unwelcoming (5)
14 Visual pun (5)
18 Going without garments (6)
19 Dog (seen in a parlour?) (6)
22 Food — larva (4)
23 Cook in water (4)

Solution see page 260

113

ACROSS

1 Inconstancy (10)

7 Cherished (8)

8 Swag (4)

9 Peter Pan villain (4)

10 Self-centredness (7)

12 Close together (5,2,4)

14 Minor hitches (7)

16 No-win situation? (4)

19 Hindquarters (4)

20 Bitterness (8)

21 Skulduggery (5-5)

DOWN

1 Out and away — UK shipping forecast area (5)

2 Violent windstorm (7)

3 Landlocked south-east Asian country (4)

4 Small bunches of flowers (8)

5 Burst (5)

6 Small bit of food (6)

11 Type of tuna (8)

12 Sexual intercourse (6)

13 Rowers (7)

15 Drink of tea (informal) (5)

17 Peter Pan heroine (5)

18 Hold fast (4)

Solution see page 261

114

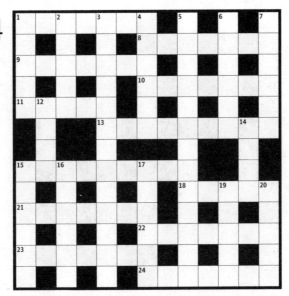

ACROSS

1 Day of rest (7)

8 City hosting the 1996 Olympics (7)

9 Fighter — bully (7)

10 (Spanish) womaniser (3,4)

11 Distinctive attitudes of a people (5)

13 Tender or romantic emotion (9)

15 Subject someone to stressful indoctrination (9)

18 I'm sad (anag) — king of Phrygia (5)

21 Spins round (7)

22 I'm so new (anag) — attractive (7)

23 Surpassed (7)

24 Defies (7)

DOWN

1 Sword (that may be rattled) (5)

2 Substantial branch of a tree (5)

3 Murder of a public figure (13)

4 Become less sympathetic (6)

5 Flattering inducements (13)

6 Far from certain (6)

7 Proverbially greedy seabird (6)

12 Norse god of thunder (4)

14 Star showing a sudden, brief increase in luminosity (4)

15 Warren (6)

16 Canny (6)

17 Solution (6)

19 Anything worthless (5)

20 Leaks slowly (5)

Solution see page 261

115

ACROSS

1 Advertising tune (6)
4 Kind of earring or bow tie (4-2)
8 Small group or team (5)
9 Extreme nervousness (7)
10 Hangs about (7)
11 Something one hopes to attain (5)
12 Forerunner (9)
17 Pungent (5)
19 Properly arranged (2,5)
21 Edible fish (7)
22 Odds? (5)
23 Perfumed hair dressing (6)
24 Lookout (6)

DOWN

1 Push and shove (6)
2 Feed (7)
3 Soup server (5)
5 Renting out (7)
6 Firearm — collector's item (5)
7 Swiss food and drink company (6)
9 Proved to be right (9)
13 Sequoia (7)
14 Beef, lamb or mutton before cooking (3,4)
15 Turn (something) down (4,2)
16 Exaggeratedly proper (6)
18 Field — kingdom (5)
20 Grossly overweight (5)

Solution see page 261

116

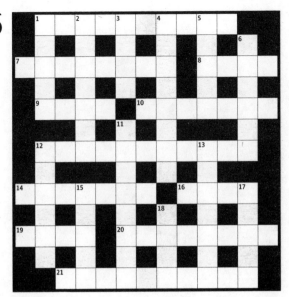

ACROSS

1 Where an outbreak of hostilities is likely (10)
7 Representative (8)
8 Fluctuate (4)
9 Antipathy (4)
10 Stiff and pompous (7)
12 Unattainable (6,5)
14 Complain (7)
16 Arrogant person (4)
19 Sharp — express grief (4)
20 Lacking knowledge and ability (informal) (8)
21 On the whole (2,3,5)

DOWN

1 Soft muscular tissue (5)
2 With skill (7)
3 Practical joke (4)
4 Capsize (8)
5 New — book (5)
6 Opening for loading a gun (6)
11 C of E (8)
12 Cereal used in brewing (6)
13 Doughnut-shaped — a LAN run (anag) (7)
15 Moth-eaten (5)
17 Tack with long, loose stitches (5)
18 Stock Exchange speculator (4)

Solution see page 261

117

ACROSS

1 Strong and sturdy (6)
4 Natty (6)
9 Choral work (7)
10 Do — political group (5)
11 Of very poor quality (5)
12 Slightly hungry (7)
13 London area with an annual carnival (7,4)
18 Small case with a shoulder strap (7)
20 Pear-shaped tropical fruit (5)
22 Restrict (5)
23 Icy (7)
24 Old-fashioned laundry appliance (6)
25 Odd or fanciful idea (6)

DOWN

1 Ornate architectural style (6)
2 Immoderate indulgence (5)
3 Remain in the same place (4,3)
5 Jelly based on fish or meat stock (5)
6 Not complete (7)
7 Cycle — cadence (6)
8 Bell-ringing (11)
14 Low stuffed seat (7)
15 Piffle (7)
16 Refuge (6)
17 On-board cooking area (6)
19 Code word for H (5)
21 Proposition assumed to be self-evident (5)

Solution see page 262

118

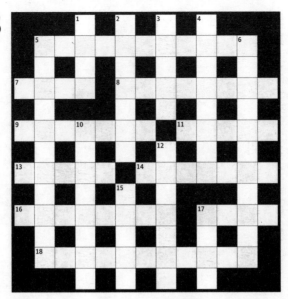

ACROSS

5 Slogan (11)
7 Weaving machine (4)
8 Game played in an alley (8)
9 Trying to make somebody believe what is not true as a joke (3-4)
11 Cruelly rapacious person (5)
13 Piece of turf dug out by a golf club (5)
14 Badly affected (4,3)
16 Accelerates (6,2)
17 Fast — food (4)
18 Damaging (11)

DOWN

1 Main upright of a ship's bow (4)
2 Hideous (7)
3 Arab leader — hikes (anag) (5)
4 Apprehended (8)
5 Reticent — saying little (5-6)
6 Shocking fish? (8,3)
10 Estate (8)
12 More joyful (7)
15 Up and about — is art (anag) (5)
17 Government tax (4)

Solution see page 262

119

ACROSS

1 Brusque (6)
4 Strong and heavy in build (5)
7 Short-legged hound (6)
8 Relating to flowers (6)
9 Foxtrot follower (4)
10 Author of The Remains of the Day (8)
12 Smelling salts (3,8)
17 Busily working (4,2,2)
19 Bird of prey (4)
20 Zigzag ski race (6)
21 Material for violin strings (6)
22 Very much (2,3)
23 Harass vocally (6)

DOWN

1 Legendary female warriors (7)
2 Soothing (7)
3 Underskirt (9)
4 Pakistani curry dish, originating perhaps in 1970s' Birmingham (5)
5 Baleen whale (7)
6 Cowardly (6)
11 Great sadness (9)
13 Amount of land (7)
14 Principal city of Siberia — UK skirt (anag) (7)
15 Express eager enjoyment (7)
16 Selected (6)
18 Shun (5)

Solution see page 262

120

ACROSS

1 Most expensive theatre seats (6)

4 Edible nut like a smooth walnut (5)

7 Give back (6)

8 Attack violently (6)

9 Person living off various dubious schemes (4)

10 Data included in cricket statistics (8)

12 Principal source of control over any complex activity (5,6)

17 Homicide (8)

19 Anger — fashion (4)

20 Sycophant (6)

21 Senselessly cruel (6)

22 Buchan's 1915 novel has 39 of them (5)

23 Traditional story (6)

DOWN

1 Wake later than intended (5,2)

2 Trembling (7)

3 Listen attentively (4,2,3)

4 Difficult question (5)

5 Warhorse (7)

6 Phrase used to emphasise admiration or surprise (2,4)

11 Extremely unpleasant (9)

13 Pain in the head (7)

14 Infliction of great suffering (7)

15 Vera Lynn was sure there would always be one (7)

16 Underwear (6)

18 Fifty-fifty (5)

Solution see page 262

121

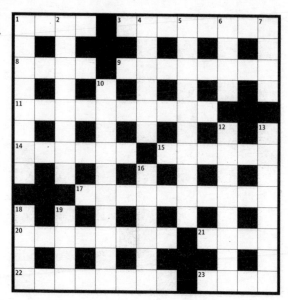

ACROSS

1 Celebrity (4)

3 Typewriter feature, used to achieve capital letters (5,3)

8 Vow (4)

9 Itinerant state (8)

11 Beyond a normal person's power (10)

14 Immeasurably small — omit AC (anag) (6)

15 Goodness (6)

17 Sinner (10)

20 Professor retired from regular work (8)

21 Dull sound of something hitting the ground (4)

22 Approach (4,4)

23 Semicircular end of a church, behind the altar (4)

DOWN

1 Old writing paper size — cops loaf (anag) (8)

2 Figure of speech (8)

4 Break — respite (6)

5 Cow, sheep or chicken? (4,6)

6 Bend or twist (4)

7 Toy consisting of a spool and string (2-2)

10 Watering (10)

12 Unfairly organised situation (6-2)

13 Give resentfully (8)

16 Cloud of gas and dust in outer space (6)

18 Leash — Pb (4)

19 Welsh actress, Catherine ___-Jones, b. 1969 (4)

Solution see page 263

122

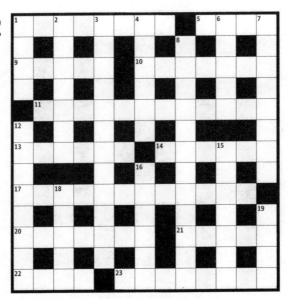

ACROSS

1 Timidity preventing further action (4,4)

5 Spanish "champagne" (4)

9 Mum's brother (5)

10 Plants with showy coloured flowers from Mexico and Central America (7)

11 Quickly and in large amounts (4,4,4)

13 Ancient (3-3)

14 Lack of foresight? (6)

17 Change completely in appearance (12)

20 Hybrid between grapefruit and mandarin (7)

21 A comfortable corner? (5)

22 Gentle and submissive (4)

23 Check text for accuracy (4-4)

DOWN

1 The heart of the matter (4)

2 Breastfeed (7)

3 Binoculars (5,7)

4 Salad plant with bitter leaves (6)

6 Excuse for not doing something (5)

7 Breed of large dogs used in police work (8)

8 Sweet, dark red liqueur (6,6)

12 General servant (8)

15 Piously solemn (2-5)

16 Balkan province that declared independence from Serbia in 2008 (6)

18 Little orphan of a Broadway musical (not the one with a gun!) (5)

19 Went — radically inclined (4)

Solution see page 263

123

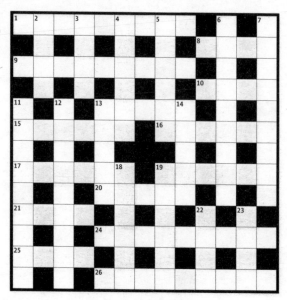

ACROSS

1 Established way of working (9)
8 The American Tribal Love–Rock Musical (1967) (4)
9 Beautify spuriously (9)
10 Part of a necklace (4)
13 Fruit of the blackthorn (5)
15 Impertinent (6)
16 Aligns (anag) — gesture (6)
17 Sudden violent wind (6)
19 Show off (6)
20 Cash (slang) (5)
21 Act — exploit (4)
24 Very hot (9)
25 Location (4)
26 Flexibility (9)

DOWN

2 Irritate (4)
3 Arrive (4)
4 In an ominous way (6)
5 Moves hastily (6)
6 Gaping (9)
7 Tendency to believe anything (9)
11 Support financially (9)
12 Ornamental shoulder pad (9)
13 Calm — even so (5)
14 Ludicrous (5)
18 Disreputable in a rakish sort of way (6)
19 Ruddy (6)
22 Narrow (4)
23 Snug (anag) — wildebeest (4)

Solution see page 263

124

ACROSS

1 Teases (informal) (4)
3 Give thought to (8)
9 Put forward (7)
10 Readily available (2,3)
11 One eating out (5)
12 Magnitude — scope (6)
14 Not before a stated time (2,3,8)
17 Grass-cutting implement (6)
19 Exclude — bread (anag) (5)
22 Left hungry (5)
23 Subtlety in handling difficult situations (7)
24 Put up with (8)
25 Greenish-blue colour (4)

DOWN

1 Left over (8)
2 Started (5)
4 Seemingly (2,3,4,2,2)
5 Member of the weasel family (5)
6 Easing of hostility between nations (7)
7 Tears (4)
8 Legally binding decision (6)
13 Fish providing isinglass (8)
15 Diplomatic (7)
16 Cargo (6)
18 English royal house (5)
20 Disagreeably domineering (5)
21 Only — fair (4)

Solution see page 263

125

ACROSS

1 Penal institution where inmates are forced to work (6,4)
7 Fall asleep (4,3)
8 Encrypted (5)
10 A smaller amount (4)
11 Type of tooth (8)
13 Jewish salutation (6)
15 Graduate's qualification (6)
17 Surround (8)
18 Loose scrum — handle roughly (4)
21 Chinese secret society (5)
22 Benny ___ , "King of Swing" (7)
23 Remember and take into account (4,2,4)

DOWN

1 Physical appearance (5)
2 Floating marker (4)
3 Spread out (6)
4 Salad vegetable (8)
5 Busybody (7)
6 Young person (10)
9 High-quality tea grown in northern India (10)
12 Passageway (8)
14 Collection of documents (7)
16 Connect to power supply (4,2)
19 Carrying a weapon (5)
20 Cartoon bear (4)

Solution see page 264

126

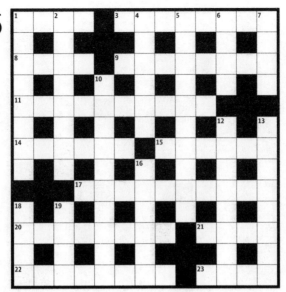

ACROSS

1 Get — derive (4)
3 Believable (8)
8 Brilliant and notable success (4)
9 Type of paint (8)
11 Encircled (10)
14 North American mountain lion (6)
15 Rush wildly (6)
17 Not showing any strain (10)
20 Recklessly resolute (4-4)
21 Arm or leg (4)
22 Trailblazers (8)
23 Major Barbara playwright (4)

DOWN

1 Backpack (8)
2 Fish tank (8)
4 North-east Italian Adriatic resort (6)
5 Soft Italian cheese (10)
6 Allurement (4)
7 Sea eagle (4)
10 Strength of character (5,5)
12 Pessimistic Old Testament prophet (8)
13 Weapon firing bolts (8)
16 Woodworker (6)
18 Vessel that carries passengers or freight (4)
19 As well (4)

Solution see page 264

127

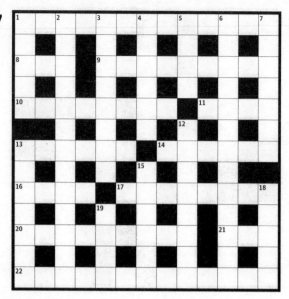

ACROSS

1 Endure misfortune stoically (4,3,4,2)
8 Donkey (3)
9 Lewdness — epic rerun (anag) (9)
10 Islands off Land's End (8)
11 Expensive brown fur (4)
13 Stripped the skin off a body (6)
14 Fried cake of minced beef served in a bun (6)
16 Centre around which something rotates (4)
17 Small marine food fish (8)
20 Sociable (9)
21 Gratuity (3)
22 Elderly internet users (6,7)

DOWN

1 Objectives (5)
2 Encouraging motivation (13)
3 Horrified (8)
4 Carelessly painted (6)
5 Islamic ruler (4)
6 Continuing skirmish (7,6)
7 One hiking long distances (7)
12 Powerfully built (8)
13 Patron saint of animals (7)
15 Fingers and toes (6)
18 Cheats (5)
19 Better half (4)

Solution see page 264

128

ACROSS

1 Small stone (6)
4 Tangled (6)
8 Implement for removing hair (5)
9 Sediment (7)
10 Acrobats' swing (7)
11 Wash — clean (5)
12 Moral decline (9)
17 Investor in a theatrical venture (5)
19 Heartache (7)
21 Harsh, shrill cry (7)
22 Cow's stomach used as food (5)
23 Fill with apprehension (6)
24 Scrounge (6)

DOWN

1 Faultlessness (6)
2 Raptor (7)
3 Big (5)
5 Anti–inflammatory tablet (7)
6 World heavyweight boxing champion, b. 1966 (5)
7 Vacillate (6)
9 Cease to be popular (3,1,5)
13 Large volcanic crater — lead car (anag) (7)
14 Particular version of a published text (7)
15 Out of date (6)
16 Dairy product (6)
18 Impales in beastly fashion (5)
20 Clobber (3–2)

Solution see page 264

129

ACROSS

1 Detroit music? (6)
4 Old European gold coin (5)
7 North Borneo sultanate (6)
8 Spun threads (6)
9 Promenade over water (4)
10 Deep blue (8)
12 Box buried today to be found some time in the future (4,7)
17 Acting as psychotherapy (4,4)
19 Green shot (4)
20 Electrics (6)
21 First in to bat (6)
22 Alpine song (5)
23 One of little importance — ante up (anag) (6)

DOWN

1 Communist (7)
2 Wobbly (7)
3 Delicately playful (9)
4 Sag (5)
5 US female working cattle (7)
6 Computer — medicine (6)
11 Young romance (5,4)
13 Boorish (3–4)
14 Numerous (7)
15 Implore (7)
16 Muscular (6)
18 Team of judges (5)

Solution see page 265

130

ACROSS

1 Place of uproar and confusion (6)
4 Short expression (6)
8 Scene of open conflict (5)
9 Human beings collectively (7)
10 Dry white Burgundy (7)
11 Beer (5)
12 Vehicle which is potentially very dangerous (9)
17 Local intonation (5)
19 Colourful parade (7)
21 Weepy (and intoxicated?) (7)
22 Mistreatment (5)
23 Lure (6)
24 Smooth and shining (6)

DOWN

1 Substance used for whitening military belts etc (6)
2 One who sticks to traditional views (7)
3 Be of service to (5)
5 Someone who directs the activities of a spy (7)
6 Taking off (5)
7 Bear without giving up (6)
9 Badly formed (9)
13 Very beautiful (7)
14 Paltry sum of money (7)
15 Thwart — my ties (anag) (6)
16 Determined (6)
18 Fully grown (5)
20 Knot in a tree (5)

Solution see page 265

131

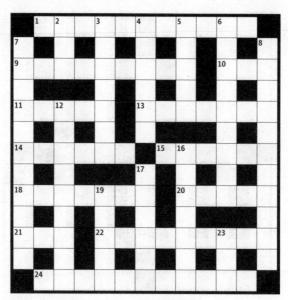

ACROSS

1 Cheerfully irresponsible (5–6)
9 Not informed (2,3,4)
10 Sheep's cry (3)
11 Divide by two (5)
13 Track by a canal (7)
14 Incite (6)
15 Dealer (6)
18 Cattle thief (7)
20 Pertaining to the period 1485–1603 (5)
21 George Gershwin's lyricist brother (3)
22 Former naval base in the Orkney Islands (5,4)
24 Means of checking horizontality (6,5)

DOWN

2 Fitting (3)
3 Ineffectual (7)
4 Small crude dwelling (6)
5 Wonky (5)
6 Scolded (9)
7 Perfectly fit and well (5,2,4)
8 GK Chesterton's detective (6,5)
12 Be quick (4,5)
16 Competitive routine with no time to relax (3,4)
17 Chicken portion (6)
19 Defeated contestant (5)
23 Be in a horizontal position (3)

Solution see page 265

132

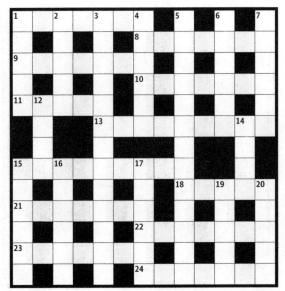

ACROSS

1 After 1918 or 1945? (4–3)
8 Fly people or goods to places not otherwise accessible (7)
9 Coach – item of footwear (7)
10 All together (2,5)
11 African wallower (abbr) (5)
13 Line showing maximum flood level (9)
15 Hurtful (9)
18 Punctuation mark (5)
21 Anticipate (7)
22 Gun (7)
23 Serving no purpose (7)
24 Hinged part of a plane's wing (7)

DOWN

1 Tone — football field (5)
2 Keen — exactly (5)
3 Shop front display organiser (6–7)
4 Most infrequent (6)
5 Post-infancy educational establishment (7,6)
6 Catnap (6)
7 Smear — run naked (6)
12 Fe — golf club (4)
14 Space (4)
15 Inundation (6)
16 Top — cow (6)
17 Black Sea port (6)
19 Car (5)
20 Pinny — part of the fairway leading up to the green (5)

Solution see page 265

133

ACROSS

1 Tightly grouped (7)
8 Spread equally (4,3)
9 Contumely (7)
10 One seeking retribution (7)
11 Attempt to fool someone (3-2)
13 Extremely wet (9)
15 Gorgeous (9)
18 Musical composition for eight performers (5)
21 Compensation for loss or injury (7)
22 Creative intellectual (7)
23 Indiscriminate slaughter (7)
24 Without affectation (7)

DOWN

1 Trainee — acted (anag) (5)
2 Foggy (5)
3 Illegal (7,3,3)
4 Lessee (6)
5 One studying weather and climate (13)
6 Leave behind unintentionally (6)
7 Squirrelled away (6)
12 Ascend (4)
14 River rising in the Czech Republic and flowing into the North Sea (4)
15 Soup made with beetroot (6)
16 Dreads (anag) — snakes (6)
17 Fix — make tight (6)
19 Person accepting an offer (5)
20 Alpine region of Austria and Italy (5)

Solution see page 266

134

ACROSS

5 Very steep (11)
7 High point (4)
8 Abnormally powerful person (8)
9 Relief (7)
11 Spicy Mexican sauce (5)
13 Landing stage (5)
14 Unoccupied post (7)
16 Curved, like an eagle's beak (8)
17 Bung — promotion (4)
18 Student of races and peoples (11)

DOWN

1 Celebrate (4)
2 Sticky (7)
3 Ancient Roman country house (5)
4 Greek minced lamb dish (8)
5 Pretty — quaint (11)
6 Indoor ball game venue — SAS cut our HQ (anag) (6,5)
10 Scrap between women (8)
12 Place where King Arthur held court (7)
15 Swivel (5)
17 Bucket (4)

Solution see page 266

135

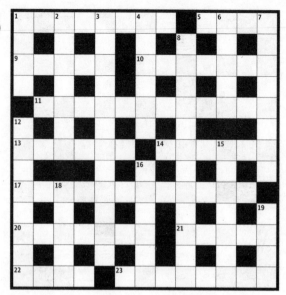

ACROSS

1 Social networking website (8)
5 Gait between a walk and a canter (4)
9 East African country (5)
10 Dante's tongue (7)
11 Administrative centre (12)
13 What's yet to come (6)
14 Darwin voyaged in this ship (6)
17 Revolt (12)
20 Pernickety (7)
21 Approach — disagreement (3-2)
22 Stone (4)
23 Incarcerate (8)

DOWN

1 Sham (4)
2 Nunnery (7)
3 Common brown seaweed (12)
4 Detestable (6)
6 Lift up (5)
7 Chemical element, symbol W (8)
8 Cure for balding? (4,8)
12 Michelle ___ , US movie star (8)
15 Coffee sediment (7)
16 Heavy cream-coloured writing paper (6)
18 Relating to sound (5)
19 By and by (4)

Solution see page 266

136

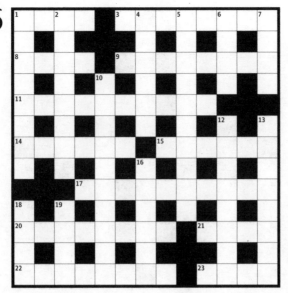

ACROSS

1 Criminal association (4)

3 Result of division (8)

8 Well ventilated (4)

9 Fitful (8)

11 Southern African plant of the lily family — haunts a gap (anag) (10)

14 Company of performers (6)

15 Italian ice cream (6)

17 Dressing like mayonnaise (5,5)

20 Baby's onesie (8)

21 Aquatic bird with short legs (4)

22 Indian or Chinese, for those who don't want to cook (8)

23 All right (4)

DOWN

1 Agreement to answer for another's debts (8)

2 Teller (8)

4 Bumptious (6)

5 Upheaval (10)

6 Whirling current (4)

7 Bloodsucking arachnid (4)

10 World's largest inland body of water, fed by the Volga River (7,3)

12 Person with rapidly declining power (4,4)

13 In a usual situation (8)

16 Sheen produced by age and polishing (6)

18 Predicament (4)

19 Pull sharply (4)

Solution see page 266

137

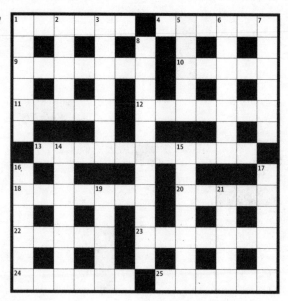

ACROSS

1 Technical researcher (6)
4 No longer open (6)
9 Resolute in the face of pain — austere (7)
10 Land attached to a parish church (5)
11 Punctuation mark (5)
12 Presume — rue miss (anag) (7)
13 Uninvited guest (11)
18 Disconcerted (7)
20 Burst open (5)
22 System of religious principles (5)
23 Put on a pedestal (7)
24 Impressionist painter of British nationality, d. 1899 (6)
25 Plato's birthplace (6)

DOWN

1 Essential principles (6)
2 Weak and delicate (5)
3 Deeply emotional (7)
5 German pistol (5)
6 Incapable of reproducing (7)
7 Make stronger (6)
8 Filled with a feeling of dread (5-6)
14 Stag's crowning glory (7)
15 Have qualms about (7)
16 Spring-flowering plant (6)
17 Emotional tension (6)
19 Long-handled spoon (5)
21 Rent — easel (anag) (5)

Solution see page 267

138

ACROSS

1 Have the opposite and damaging effect to that intended (8)

5 (When citing a reference) in the same place (abbr) (4)

9 Popular dance music of the 1970s (5)

10 Thick sugar paste used for icing cakes (7)

11 Person in their sixties (12)

13 Orion — pocket watch with a hinged protective lid (6)

14 Nocturnal wild cat of Central and South America (6)

17 Noisily aggressive (12)

20 Rotary engine (7)

21 Wide — impenetrable (5)

22 Panache (4)

23 Log store (8)

DOWN

1 Cots, bunks etc — eastern English county (abbr) (4)

2 Toilet water reservoir (7)

3 Soft fresh cheese, like thick yogurt (7,5)

4 Automatic action (6)

6 Indian dish consisting of vegetables deep fried in batter (5)

7 Explode (8)

8 Banged up (12)

12 Song thrush — short let (anag) (8)

15 Uncouth (7)

16 Swimming briefs trademark (6)

18 Middle East country, capital Damascus (5)

19 Slide out of control (4)

Solution see page 267

139

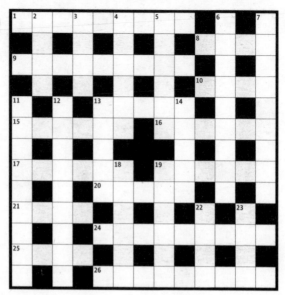

ACROSS

1 Entrance hall — foyer (9)
8 Shed tears (4)
9 Open to argument (9)
10 Fruit (4)
13 Capital of Western Australia (5)
15 Earnest request (6)
16 Centres (6)
17 Small ornamental case worn on a chain (6)
19 Small pointed beard (6)
20 Mountain ash (5)
21 Involving bloodshed (4)
24 Interesting phenomenon — show (9)
25 Part of a shoe (4)
26 Made extremely sad (9)

DOWN

2 Organs of sight (4)
3 Hard durable timber (4)
4 Dam-building rodent (6)
5 Adam's first wife? — Frasier Crane's second ex-wife (6)
6 Make merry (9)
7 Downtrodden (9)
11 Ask forgiveness (9)
12 Gondolier's song (9)
13 Dwindle away to nothing (5)
14 Grey or white wading bird (5)
18 Small hairpiece to cover bald patch (6)
19 Cowboy of the pampas (6)
22 Coffee — programming language (4)
23 Adhesive (4)

Solution see page 267

140

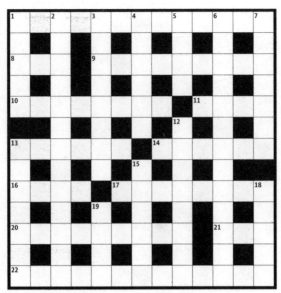

ACROSS

1 Bowl-shaped aerial (9,4)

8 Tavern (3)

9 Got rid of (9)

10 Moment of sudden revelation (involving three wise men from the east?) (8)

11 Preminger or von Bismarck? (4)

13 Globule full of gas (6)

14 Polecat bred for hunting rats and rabbits (6)

16 Chess piece — puppet (4)

17 Natural margin on the head (that recedes) (8)

20 Slow (9)

21 Atmosphere (3)

22 Collection of undesirables (6,7)

DOWN

1 Malinger (5)

2 Alley game (6,7)

3 Flaw in the law? (8)

4 Young child (6)

5 Love god (4)

6 Unspecified (13)

7 Remote place used by those on the run (7)

12 Treachery (8)

13 Involving manic episodes (7)

15 Rotten scoundrel! (3,3)

18 Before the due time (5)

19 Join or blend to form an entity (4)

Solution see page 267

141

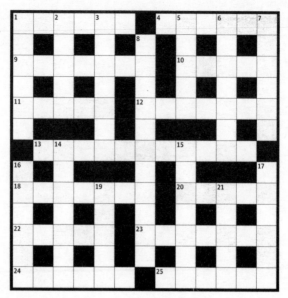

ACROSS

1 Chirping insect (6)
4 Bolshoi Ballet base (6)
9 Person born between 23 October and 22 November? (7)
10 Ventured (5)
11 Vichyssoise ingredient (5)
12 Capital of Armenia (7)
13 Weed on a moon (anag) — early spring-flowering plant (4,7)
18 Foes (7)
20 Scandalise (5)
22 Big band dance music (5)
23 Immortal (7)
24 Places of interest for tourists (6)
25 Sartre (anag) — check (6)

DOWN

1 Dear (6)
2 Identical copy (5)
3 Forcibly removed from office (7)
5 Requisition (5)
6 Mobile home (7)
7 Walking through shallow water (6)
8 One's entire self (4,3,4)
14 Job opportunity (7)
15 Wander — wind about (7)
16 Parts of a poem (6)
17 Minor — snub (6)
19 Bullion bar (5)
21 Coolness and composure under strain (5)

Solution see page 268

142

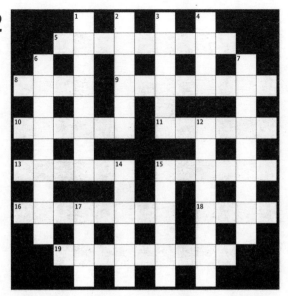

ACROSS

5 Dental problem (9)

8 Lie in the sunshine (4)

9 Beautiful character with long hair in a Brothers Grimm fairy tale, 1812 (8)

10 Regular income from employment (6)

11 Light-sensitive membrane of the eyeball (6)

13 Characteristic of the Celts (6)

15 Unwell (6)

16 Seasickness (3,2,3)

18 Flexed — penchant (4)

19 Loth (9)

DOWN

1 Harvey Wallbanger, for example (8)

2 Floor of a building (6)

3 Destitute person (6)

4 Part of the face (on which one may have to take it?) (4)

6 Boat with two hulls (9)

7 1967 Beatles' song (5,4)

12 Brass band instrument (8)

14 Enter (4,2)

15 Dangers (6)

17 Have a meal (4)

Solution see page 268

143

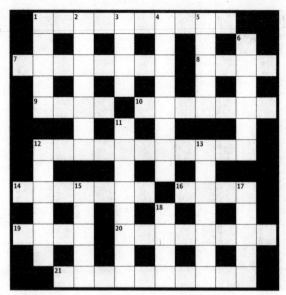

ACROSS

1 Lack of affectation or pretence (10)
7 Declare formally (8)
8 Yemeni port (4)
9 Brief look (4)
10 Homeless woman (3,4)
12 French railway (6,2,3)
14 Balkan country (7)
16 Umbrella (4)
19 O (4)
20 Waste water (8)
21 Bosom companion (4,6)

DOWN

1 Waste (5)
2 Large heavy knife for cutting vegetation (7)
3 Jump (4)
4 Soldier trained for raiding (8)
5 Rough path (5)
6 One way to get a goal in football (6)
11 Assiduous (8)
12 Person on the line (6)
13 Special attraction (7)
15 Got out of bed (5)
17 Became ill with longing (5)
18 Distant parts (4)

Solution see page 268

144

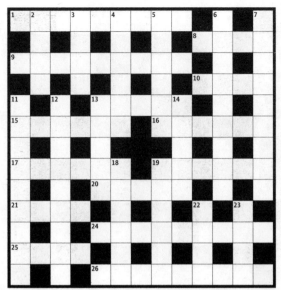

ACROSS

1 To a sickening extent (2,7)
8 Duplicate (4)
9 Olden days (9)
10 Dexterous (4)
13 South Wales town —
boy's name (5)
15 Czech composer, d. 1904 (6)
16 Calm and composed (6)
17 Regularly recurring (6)
19 Less remote (6)
20 Beautician's establishment (5)
21 In every detail (2,1,1)
24 In an unhurried manner (2,7)
25 Finished — as a remainder (4)
26 Ordained ministers (9)

DOWN

2 Ding's partner? (4)
3 Capital of Samoa (4)
4 Pip's partner — quakes (anag) (6)
5 Thespians (6)
6 Become discouraged (4,5)
7 Participant in the gunfight at
the OK Corral (5,4)
11 Academy's aim (9)
12 Hidden (9)
13 Foundation (5)
14 Middle East country (5)
18 Market-controlling
combination (6)
19 Certainly not (informal) (2,4)
22 Children's game (1,3)
23 Gaelic (4)

Solution see page 268

145

ACROSS

1 Before anything else (5,2,3)
7 Pasta envelopes with savoury filling (7)
8 Insipid — uninteresting (5)
10 Indifferent (2-2)
11 Pitmen (8)
13 Highwayman, for example (6)
15 Commotion (6)
17 Shabby (8)
18 Open pastry filled with fruit (4)
21 Live in (5)
22 Facility for use without leaving one's car (5-2)
23 Under way (2,8)

DOWN

1 Court game (5)
2 Chess piece (4)
3 Rialto (anag) — adjust to a specific need (6)
4 Extremely pleasing (8)
5 Remove one's grip (5,2)
6 Disappointingly unsuccessful (10)
9 Unobtrusively perceptive (10)
12 Dealer in precious stones (8)
14 In the space separating two objects (7)
16 Old, experienced sailor (3,3)
19 Ogles (5)
20 Code word for M (4)

Solution see page 269

146

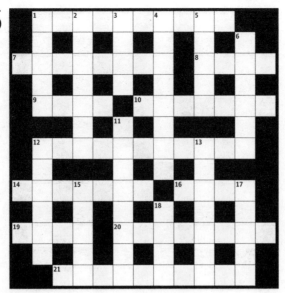

ACROSS

1 Almond-flavoured jelly-like milk pudding (10)

7 Fish — stumble helplessly (8)

8 Coal or gas? (4)

9 Bark (4)

10 One able to rise from the ashes (7)

12 Unconquerable (11)

14 West Midlands county town (7)

16 Restraint (4)

19 Two ducks in one game of cricket (4)

20 Long run (8)

21 Large, thick-skinned ungulate (10)

DOWN

1 Under (5)

2 Dissolved in water (7)

3 Surrender (4)

4 Hardy breed of Scottish dairy cattle (8)

5 Blunder (5)

6 Country formerly called British Honduras (6)

11 Astronaut (8)

12 Sort of (2,1,3)

13 Talk aggressively to little or no effect (7)

15 Value (5)

17 Foreheads (5)

18 Large, bony-plated reptile (abbr) (4)

Solution see page 269

147

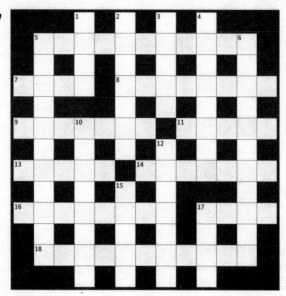

ACROSS

5 Weaponless self-defence sports (7,4)

7 Unusually large (4)

8 Computer files printed out on paper (4,4)

9 More irritating (7)

11 Far beyond the norm (5)

13 Frivolous — dizzy (5)

14 Flat heated surface used for cooking (7)

16 Serenader's tune? (4,4)

17 Podium (4)

18 Actions based on natural feelings (11)

DOWN

1 Dependable — loyal (4)

2 More suspicious (7)

3 Chat (someone) up (5)

4 With patches of light brown colour on the skin (8)

5 With high hills and crags (11)

6 Extreme excess — fruity pulse (anag) (11)

10 Bushy boundary (8)

12 Bandit (7)

15 Loot (5)

17 Podium (4)

Solution see page 269

148

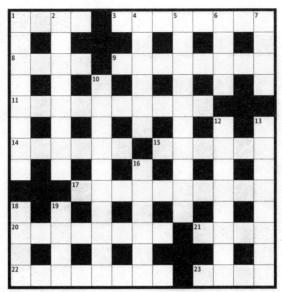

ACROSS

1 Small amount — move fast (4)
3 Intermittently (3,3,2)
8 Means of access to different floors (4)
9 Thug (8)
11 Bland — pale (5-5)
14 Motive (6)
15 Grumble (6)
17 Unkempt (10)
20 Articulate (8)
21 Restless desire (4)
22 Contemplated deeply (8)
23 Trivial quarrel (4)

DOWN

1 One of the original 13 US states (8)
2 Flattering talk (4,4)
4 With blooms (6)
5 Fashionable (3,3,4)
6 Old chief magistrate of Venice or Genoa (4)
7 Number of the ancient Muses (4)
10 Longest side of a right-angled triangle (10)
12 A period in the US! (4,4)
13 Photo showing just the face (8)
16 One of the six original members of the European Economic Community (6)
18 Army vehicle (4)
19 Satellite (4)

Solution see page 269

149

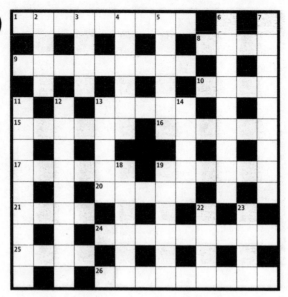

ACROSS

1 Strong artificial sweetener — same apart (anag) (9)
8 Divorce capital of Nevada (4)
9 Asian country, capital and megaport (9)
10 Berkshire public school (4)
13 Main topic of attention (5)
15 Twisting force (6)
16 Side street much used by cars in rush hours (3,3)
17 Endowed with talent (6)
19 Italian-American gangster, d. 1947 (6)
20 Run down (5)
21 Lump — sexy man (4)
24 Dirty dog (9)
25 Crotchet or minim, say? (4)
26 Fast car (or driver) (9)

DOWN

2 Propel oneself in water (4)
3 Simple, non-flowering, aquatic plant (4)
4 Move stealthily (6)
5 Mumbled expression of malcontent (6)
6 Roman leader of 100 soldiers (9)
7 In Oz, say? (4,5)
11 Theatrical props handler (9)
12 Blasphemous language (9)
13 Got furious (5)
14 Malaysian or Indonesian dish of grilled food with peanut sauce (5)
18 Hanging fold of skin on a person's neck (6)
19 Cricket pitch marking (6)
22 Drones and workers (4)
23 Semi-precious gemstone — tired old horse (4)

Solution see page 270

150

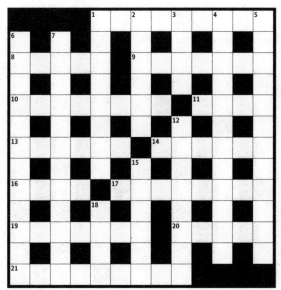

ACROSS

1 Fail to maintain contact (4,5)
8 Requirements (5)
9 First letter (7)
10 Mesmerising (8)
11 Brief and to the point (4)
13 Not presently active (6)
14 Representation of the human form (6)
16 Bearded ruminant (4)
17 Stone thrower (8)
19 Wet weather (7)
20 Russian prison camp (5)
21 Iniquitous (9)

DOWN

1 Roping (as a cowboy might) (8)
2 Hard liquor (6)
3 Dog (or part of one) (4)
4 Going everywhere (12)
5 Dominate a performance (4,3,5)
6 Gathered together in one volume (12)
7 People carrying out harmful acts (12)
12 Spreading out in different directions (8)
15 Subjected to potentially lethal fumes (6)
18 Flat tableland with steep sides (4)

Solution see page 270

151

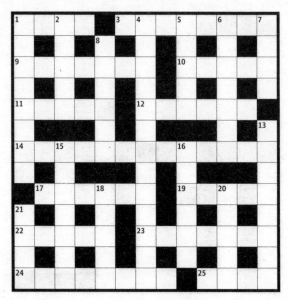

ACROSS

1 Of poor quality (4)
3 Person with a record of successes (8)
9 Pole jumper (7)
10 Two flat surfaces meeting at other than a right angle (5)
11 Phrase in a Christmas cracker (5)
12 Ultimate goal (3-3)
14 Undemanding popular music (4,9)
17 Each (6)
19 Centre (5)
22 Prize (5)
23 Tool with a wooden handle and a heavy curved metal head (7)
24 Avid reader (8)
25 And the rest (abbr) (2,2)

DOWN

1 Month (8)
2 Apples and pears etc (5)
4 Floor cleaner (6,7)
5 Retired? (2,3)
6 Venetian composer, d. 1741 (7)
7 Small rounded bread (4)
8 Leisurely walk (6)
13 Paint that dries with a sheen (8)
15 Highest female voice (7)
16 Consequence of some previous happening (6)
18 Give qualities (to) (5)
20 Where the land and sea meet (5)
21 Tender sheep meat (4)

Solution see page 270

152

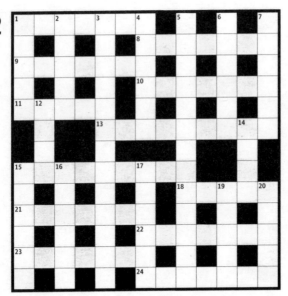

ACROSS

1 Attack with missiles (7)

8 One more (7)

9 Yellow viscous oil from animals — in on all (anag) (7)

10 Origin — see sign (anag) (7)

11 Decorate (5)

13 Salutations (9)

15 First capital of Australia (1901-27) (9)

18 Quick — reckless (5)

21 Legislator — treason (anag) (7)

22 Copy — reach equality with (7)

23 Greek goddess of the hunt (7)

24 Struggled in a confused way (7)

DOWN

1 Strong lightweight wood (5)

2 Large oval tropical fruit (5)

3 Soon enough (3,2,4,4)

4 Hang — Glenda (anag) (6)

5 Be impatient for time to pass (5,3,5)

6 Elected (6)

7 Decisive moment (6)

12 Catnap (4)

14 Special aptitude (4)

15 Lose (6)

16 Object's longest dimension (6)

17 Sartre (anag) — most uncommon (6)

19 Play for time (5)

20 Return on investment (5)

Solution see page 270

153

ACROSS

1 Cords used to close bags (11)
9 Working (9)
10 Tree with cones (3)
11 Oscillate — jazz style (5)
13 US Senate and House of Representatives building (7)
14 Salad leaves — move at great speed (6)
15 Loud noise (6)
18 Daliesque (7)
20 Echo sounder — arson (anag) (5)
21 Drink — meal (3)
22 FIFA World Cup winners in 1978 and 1986 (9)
24 Abstainer (11)

DOWN

2 Kind of whiskey (3)
3 Angry dispute (7)
4 Short, jerky motion (6)
5 Freeze over (3,2)
6 Card exchanged for goods (4,5)
7 Something hideous (11)
8 Characteristic of the working class (11)
12 Represented in bodily form (9)
16 Football club based at the Emirates Stadium (7)
17 Deliberate discourteous act (6)
19 Pass into law (5)
23 Fury (3)

Solution see page 271

154

ACROSS

1 Bright yellow flowering shrub (9)

8 Gangling (5)

9 German state and largest port (7)

10 Deep glacial crack (8)

11 Mediterranean appetisers (4)

13 XI (6)

14 Mourner carrying the coffin at a funeral (6)

16 Settled the bill (4)

17 Total forgetfulness — limbo (8)

19 Utter tremulous sounds (7)

20 Crinkled fabric — thin pancake (5)

21 Mankind (5,4)

DOWN

1 Sticky insect trap (8)

2 Use again (changing little) (6)

3 Edible tubers from the tropics (4)

4 (Of pets) not making a mess indoors (5-7)

5 Handheld power tool — Greenland rig (anag) (5,7)

6 22-yard strip between the wickets (7,5)

7 Before noon (4,8)

12 Nothing special (8)

15 Spain and Portugal (6)

18 Knock senseless (4)

Solution see page 271

155

ACROSS

1 Unreal — gorgeous (6)
4 Person moving abroad (6)
9 Biking trick (7)
10 Sulky type (5)
11 Old stringed instruments (5)
12 Bare from the waist up (7)
13 Where volunteers supply food to the homeless (4,7)
18 Quivering musical effect (7)
20 Beauty — young larva (5)
22 Consecrate (5)
23 Howl loudly (7)
24 Being (6)
25 Spirited — argumentative (6)

DOWN

1 Festival in honour of Lakshmi (6)
2 Use (5)
3 Unassertive male person (7)
5 Swot (3,2)
6 Holey cheese (7)
7 Reveal (6)
8 Voice-throwing technique (11)
14 Gorge oneself (7)
15 Perform magic tricks (7)
16 Fixed (6)
17 Breathing in laboured manner (6)
19 Beginning (of something unpleasant?) (5)
21 Resources (5)

Solution see page 271

156

ACROSS

1 US state, joined 1861 (6)
4 Herb with prickly flower heads — elates (anag) (6)
9 Lover (7)
10 Droll — suspicious (5)
11 Yellow-orange colour (5)
12 Ordinary (7)
13 US state, joined 1817 (11)
18 Chinese breed of small dog (4-3)
20 Disney's flying elephant (5)
22 Comic — party (5)
23 Salve (7)
24 Get-up-and-go (6)
25 Panorama (6)

DOWN

1 Warning horn (6)
2 Voluptuously beautiful young woman (5)
3 Stifling (7)
5 Small and delicate (5)
6 Bronzer? (7)
7 Non-professionals (6)
8 Dissolute (11)
14 Take off (7)
15 Alphabetical listings (7)
16 Functioning (6)
17 Poetic fourteen-liner (6)
19 G-string (5)
21 Corncob plant (5)

Solution see page 271

157

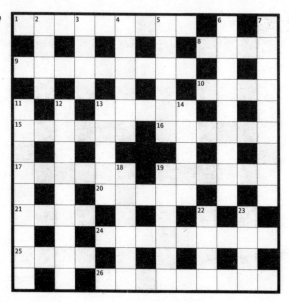

ACROSS

1 Thankfulness (9)
8 Fly high (4)
9 Near thing (5,4)
10 Plant growing where it is not wanted (4)
13 Fundamental belief (5)
15 Tasty morsel (6)
16 Stymie (6)
17 Deranged person (6)
19 Mouth of a volcano (6)
20 Starkers (5)
21 Ms Locket? (4)
24 Recover consciousness (4,5)
25 Central point (4)
26 Expose to a current of fresh air (9)

DOWN

2 Bap (4)
3 Assignment (4)
4 Price label (6)
5 Pleasing to the ear (6)
6 Sample of something that lies ahead (9)
7 Killing and feeding on others (9)
11 Study of the origins of words (9)
12 Regardless of the price (2,3,4)
13 Saturn's largest satellite (5)
14 Last place on the podium? (5)
18 Inveigle (6)
19 Building material (6)
22 Covering for a chimney (4)
23 This month (abbr) (4)

Solution see page 272

158

ACROSS

1 Hurry up! (3,1,4,2)
7 Long narrow flags (8)
8 Unbridgeable disparity (4)
9 Near (4)
10 Sweet sauce made with milk and eggs (7)
12 Device for dispersing a crowd (5,6)
14 Native of Flanders (7)
16 Part of the eye (4)
19 Owl's cry (4)
20 Made better (8)
21 Author of Dracula (4,6)

DOWN

1 Putting area (5)
2 This evening (7)
3 Trappist, for example (4)
4 Relating to blood vessels (8)
5 Should (5)
6 Old two-shilling coin (6)
11 Favouritism shown to friends and associates (8)
12 Tree providing wood for cricket bats (6)
13 English county (7)
15 Mother (Latin) (5)
17 Guide — bullock (5)
18 Blob (4)

Solution see page 272

159

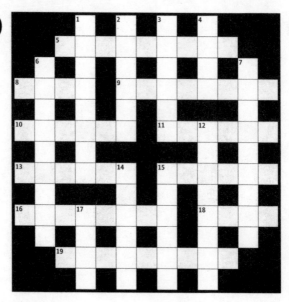

ACROSS

5,19 All over the place (4,5,3,6)
8 Clarified butter used in Indian cookery (4)
9 Royal attendant (8)
10 Uncompromising (6)
11 Delivery note (6)
13 Situation causing delay (4–2)
15 Treat with contempt (6)
16 Large animal (in the room?) (8)
18 Kind of sugar? (4)
19 See 5

DOWN

1 Put back (8)
2 Short and solid (6)
3 Fluid (6)
4 Scarcely detectable amount (4)
6,7 I won't divulge the information! (4,5,2,7)
12 Kind of plastic? (8)
14 Flatfish (6)
15 Meaning — determined (6)
17 Gamble — boat — high kick (4)

Solution see page 272

160

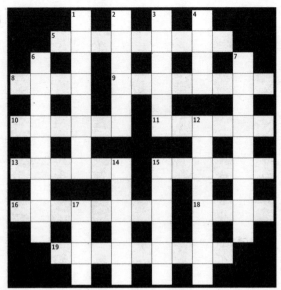

ACROSS

5 Exhausted (slang) (9)
8 One of the Channel Islands (4)
9 Inherent ability (8)
10 Marine reptile (6)
11 Wealth (6)
13 Sagacity (6)
15 Ecclesiastical area (6)
16 Elated (8)
18 Untainted (4)
19 Flawed (9)

DOWN

1 Lively (8)
2 Abrasion — predicament (6)
3 Divine drink (6)
4 Zone — thrash (4)
6 Pulchritudinous (9)
7 Opponent (9)
12 Hard shell (8)
14 Homicide (6)
15 Appease (6)
17 Domicile (4)

Solution see page 272

161

ACROSS

1 Meaning the same (10)

7 Travelling at less than Mach 1 (8)

8 Classical (abbr) (4)

9 Murder (2,2)

10 Feverish (7)

12 Likely to drop off at any moment (11)

14 Orinoco, Wellington, Bulgaria etc (7)

16 Cattle meat (4)

19 Potter's furnace (4)

20 Majestic — spacious (8)

21 Idiot — haunted Tom (anag) (10)

DOWN

1 Healthy (5)

2 More disgusting (7)

3 Idiot (4)

4 Food fish (8)

5 Make sounds (but not necessarily words) (5)

6 Bulbous herb used in cooking (6)

11 Enticing source of pleasure (8)

12 Sex (slang) (6)

13 Framework to support a flat surface — letters (anag) (7)

15 Group of widely spoken languages of southern Africa (5)

17 Duplicity (5)

18 Baked dish filled with fruit or custard (4)

Solution see page 273

162

ACROSS

1 Loving touch (6)

4 Fragment of pottery (5)

7 Landlocked country of south central Africa (6)

8 American country — eco-mix (anag) (6)

9 Serious falling out (4)

10 Store through which you are forced to pass on the way out? (4,4)

12 Spongy confection, often toasted (11)

17 Cost (5,3)

19 Ship's company (4)

20 Country — 21 shillings (6)

21 Ready and wanting to have children (6)

22 Minuscule (5)

23 Boil (with anger?) (6)

DOWN

1 Skull (7)

2 Nuclear energy generator (7)

3 Catapult — thin gloss (anag) (9)

4 American clay pigeon shooting (5)

5 Sneeze sound (7)

6 Hanging loose (6)

11 Easily broken — gerbil fan (anag) (9)

13 Senseless (7)

14 Exclusion of the workforce by the management (7)

15 Deploy sweet talk (7)

16 Cask's plug (6)

18 Poem lamenting the dead (5)

Solution see page 273

163

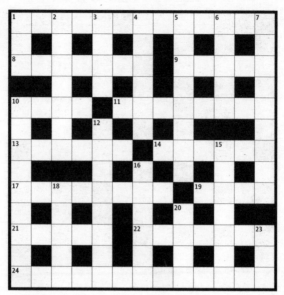

ACROSS

1 One of the original 13 colonies of the United States, capital Raleigh (5,8)

8 Pipe leaves (7)

9 Attribute (5)

10 Repeat a passage from some written work (4)

11 1940s' genre of American thriller or detective movies (French) (4,4)

13 Repeated performance demanded by an audience (6)

14 Basic — original (6)

17 Football upright (8)

19 Flakes that drift (4)

21 Close chum (slang) (5)

22 Large edible flatfish (7)

24 Cold wind in Europe — rent a hostelry (anag) (13)

DOWN

1 Fool (3)

2 Unthinking, like a machine (7)

3 Rhine wine — horse joint (4)

4 Immeasurably small (6)

5 Win by clever thinking (8)

6 Adult insect (5)

7 Pleasure of remembering something nice (9)

10 Person of the cloth (9)

12 Painting on three hinged panels (8)

15 Hotel room chiller? (7)

16 Breathing problem (6)

18 Subsequently (5)

20 Surfeit (4)

23 Rugby score (3)

Solution see page 273

164

ACROSS

5 Paint thinner (5,6)
7 Flash — bloodsucker (4)
8 Introduction (8)
9 Imposing (7)
11 Rice field (5)
13 Small coin (5)
14 A lot of runs! (7)
16 Needy — secured (8)
17 Vegetable garden — scheme (4)
18 Bedroom battle (where feathers fly?) (6,5)

DOWN

1 Cream (4)
2 Practical joke (3-4)
3 Kiss — server (5)
4 Haughty (8)
5 Fast and with only brief pauses (7-4)
6 Discharge of lightning (11)
10 Slender flexible limb (8)
12 Demonstration of good wishes before departure (4-3)
15 Ghost — US spy (5)
17 Youth acting as a knight's attendant (4)

Solution see page 273

165

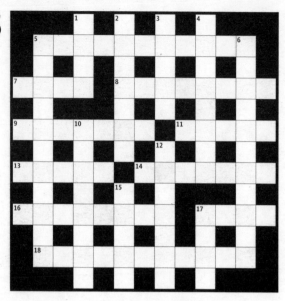

ACROSS

5 Was grateful for (11)
7 Detachment (4)
8 Attractive (8)
9 Charity worker asking for subscriptions on the street (7)
11 Mediterranean island (5)
13 Unattractive (5)
14 Old stager (7)
16 Spoken for (8)
17 Nosh (4)
18 Announcement (11)

DOWN

1 Narrow point of land projecting into the sea (4)
2 Highly excited (7)
3 Humorous (5)
4 Barrier of stakes and timbers (8)
5 Destroyed completely (11)
6 Cooked perfectly (4,2,1,4)
10 Leadership (8)
12 Forward progress (7)
15 Shoddy (5)
17 Fluent and plausible (4)

Solution see page 274

166

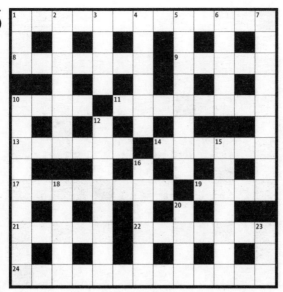

ACROSS

1 Free (13)

8 Produce a new version of a document (7)

9 First letter of the Hebrew alphabet (5)

10 Purple-brown colour (4)

11 Africa country, until 1966 called Bechuanaland (8)

13 Naval hero, d. 21 October 1805 (6)

14 Horizontal band on a wall (6)

17 Enterprising person (2-6)

19 London district known for its nightlife (4)

21 One of Chaucer's Canterbury pilgrims (5)

22 Fulminate (7)

24 Kind of 2 down treatment — temple acronym (anag) (13)

DOWN

1 Road vehicle (3)

2 Declaim (anag) — health check (7)

3 Bread — head (4)

4 Meat (that may be dressed as lamb?) (6)

5 Biblical vessel (5,3)

6 Contest venue (5)

7 Sailors' chant while hauling on ropes (2-5-2)

10 Eulogy (9)

12 Canadian city (8)

15 Art of a sexual nature (7)

16 Gas used in balloons (6)

18 Sparkle (5)

20 Like 2018 but not 2017 (4)

23 Meadow crop (3)

Solution see page 274

167

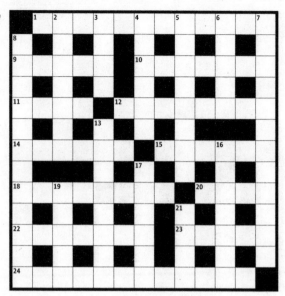

ACROSS

1 Figurative (12)
9 Muse of lyric poetry (5)
10 Deteriorate through neglect (2,2,3)
11 Either side of the backbone between the hip bone and ribs (4)
12 Distribute (8)
14 Merciful — grub (6)
15 Composer of Messiah, d. 1759 (6)
18 Imprisoned (8)
20 Weep noisily (4)
22 Sea creature with a spiral tusk (7)
23 Incendiarism (5)
24 Adventurous (12)

DOWN

2 Toenail (anag) — delight (7)
3 Highly excited (4)
4 Bargain (6)
5 Of sound mind — not a liar (anag) (8)
6 Italian-American film director of It's a Wonderful Life, d. 1991 (5)
7 Refrain from interfering with satisfactory situation (3,4,5)
8 Pugnacity (12)
13 Decisive argument (8)
16 Lasts interminably (5,2)
17 Vendor (6)
19 Deserve (5)
21 Amorous advance (4)

Solution see page 274

168

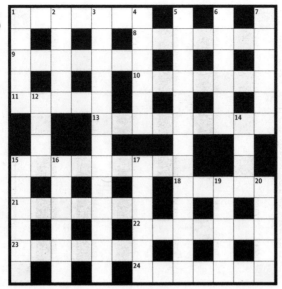

ACROSS

1 Ring shaped to line a small hole (7)

8 "Master" of "stream", say (7)

9 Related to language (7)

10 Card game — as an act (anag) (7)

11 Grating (5)

13 Adult females (9)

15 Maize (9)

18 Excited by desire (5)

21 Short passage (7)

22 Insect's body part (7)

23 Hundredth of an old Deutschmark (7)

24 A poetical tear? (3–4)

DOWN

1 Narrow gorge with a stream in North America (5)

2 One in possession (5)

3 Very tasty (5–8)

4 Powder used on the body (6)

5 Sewing tool (7,6)

6 Mural painted on wet plaster (6)

7 Set out (on an enterprise) (6)

12 State openly (4)

14 Green fruit (4)

15 Nodding off (6)

16 Top (6)

17 Temporary suspension of operation (6)

19 More spirited (5)

20 Sewed together quickly (3,2)

Solution see page 274

169

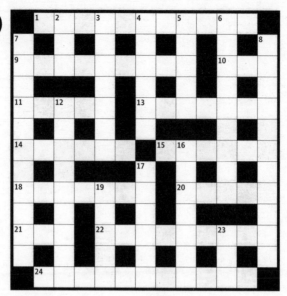

ACROSS

1 Filled to capacity (5-1-5)
9 Strenuous activity (9)
10 Our nearest star (3)
11 Come about (5)
13 Stayed longer than intended (7)
14 Rattled (6)
15 Captain Hook, say (6)
18 Cause aversion (7)
20 Short message posted on the internet (5)
21 Label (3)
22 What did you say? (4,5)
24 Filled up again (11)

DOWN

2 Shade (3)
3 Exclusive circle (7)
4 Takes over (6)
5 A failure (5)
6 Criticise severely (9)
7 Make a forceful protest (11)
8 Unintentional (11)
12 White sparkling wine (9)
16 Weeping (2,5)
17 Mariner (6)
19 From the vicinity (5)
23 Mature (3)

Solution see page 275

170

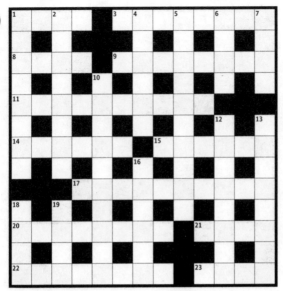

ACROSS

1 Fit of offended dignity (4)
3 Execution platform (8)
8 Delicate (and frilly?) (4)
9 Mounted bullfighter (8)
11 Rep's patter (5,5)
14 Introduce (6)
15 Make indirect reference to (6)
17 White, as a mountain top (4-6)
20 In the right way (8)
21 Power of choice of action (4)
22 Ponder (8)
23 Algae extract used as a food thickening or gelling agent (4)

DOWN

1 Emphasising the functional relation between parts and the whole (8)
2 Irresponsible (8)
4 US biscuit (6)
5 Cat's anti-pest ring (4,6)
6 Likelihood (4)
7 Road vehicle fuel (4)
10 Sour tasting (10)
12 Ball of steamed dough (8)
13 Swinging back and forth freely under gravity (8)
16 Illuminated at dusk (6)
18 Larger than life (4)
19 Hanker (4)

Solution see page 275

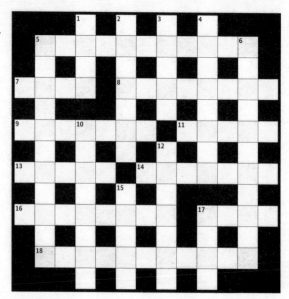

ACROSS

5 Psychic (11)
7 Depressed (4)
8 Get the better of (8)
9 Members of a coven (7)
11 Highest part in a piece of choral music — act on (anag) (5)
13 Calamari (5)
14 Small fry (7)
16 Dyspeptic (8)
17 Spiritedness (4)
18 Sparkle (11)

DOWN

1 Stark — naked (4)
2 Cavalry soldier (7)
3 Time period (5)
4 Agricultural worker (8)
5 Agree that the terms are now equal and satisfactory (4,2,5)
6 Reverse the course of events (4,3,4)
10 Principles for assessment (8)
12 With gentleness (7)
15 Unclean (5)
17 Card game (4)

Solution see page 275

172

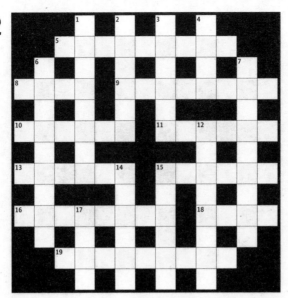

ACROSS

5 Quickly rotating mass of water (9)
8 Forehead (4)
9 Ignore (8)
10 French cake (6)
11 Raised (6)
13 Skimpy undergarments (6)
15 More difficult (6)
16 Big Apple borough (8)
18 Pulls hard (4)
19 Largest living animal (4,5)

DOWN

1 Chinese-style noodle dish (4,4)
2 Gilt or bronzed metallic ware (6)
3 Attraction — legal process (6)
4 Fee for the use of a road or bridge (4)
6 Perfidy (9)
7 Old gold coin (9)
12 Predict (8)
14 Precious metal (6)
15 Largest of the Japanese islands (6)
17 Liquids for frying (4)

Solution see page 275

173

ACROSS

1 Be good enough (4,6)
7 Recovered (7)
8 Vented (5)
10 Be absorbed in thought (4)
11 Emerging from an egg (8)
13 Realm (6)
15 Flock of geese (6)
17 Charles II's long-standing mistress (4,4)
18 Deliberately avoid (4)
21 Foreigner (5)
22 Net income (7)
23 Libellous (10)

DOWN

1 Medication (5)
2 Brief satirical sketch (4)
3 Type of curry (6)
4 Multi-media messaging app (8)
5 Item of jewellery (7)
6 Female opera star (5,5)
9 Tenacity (10)
12 One of the 13 original US states (8)
14 Out-of-sorts feeling (7)
16 Nearsightedness (6)
19 Hirsute (5)
20 Gabrielle Bonheur Chanel (4)

Solution see page 276

174

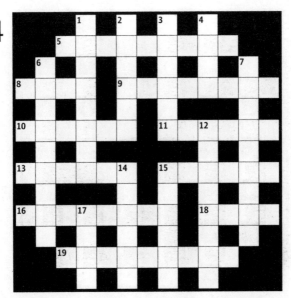

ACROSS

5 With a high opinion of oneself (9)
8 Regretted (4)
9 Sane (8)
10 Chum (6)
11 Resist (6)
13 Combined (6)
15 Irish novelist, Maeve, d. 2012 (6)
16 Winter road hazard (5,3)
18 Castle (4)
19 Incessant readers (9)

DOWN

1 Loss of nerve (4,4)
2 Coders (anag) (6)
3 Small French restaurant (6)
4 Mexican currency (4)
6 At the present time (9)
7 Lie (9)
12 Extensive view (8)
14 Imbibes (6)
15 Native of Brittany (6)
17 Profit-sharing enterprise (abbr) (2-2)

Solution see page 276

175

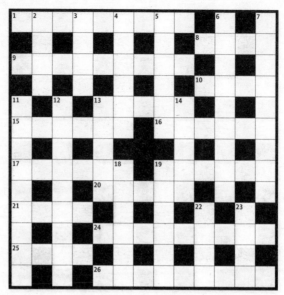

ACROSS

1 Mawkish (9)
8 Wrap-around garment for smart old Roman (4)
9 Behind the scenes (9)
10 French cheese (4)
13 Smoke from Havana! (5)
15 Latin American dance (3–3)
16 French-speaking Swiss city (6)
17 Frightening female (6)
19 Very generous (6)
20 Small firecracker (5)
21 Small South African rural town (4)
24 Flippant (9)
25 Sty noise (4)
26 Righty-ho! (4–5)

DOWN

2 Hello — goodbye (4)
3 Voice amplifier (abbr) (4)
4 Baltic country (6)
5 Go this way, then that (6)
6 Middle-class (9)
7 Unwilling to be photographed (6–3)
11 Squeeze box (9)
12 Evidence of underground fungal growth (5,4)
13 Game with a Sicilian defence (5)
14 Place of treatment for addicts (5)
18 Screech (6)
19 Special uniform (6)
22 Banking system — social security cheque (4)
23 Smart American guy (4)

Solution see page 276

176

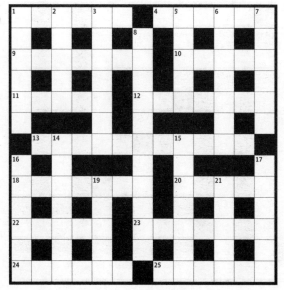

ACROSS

1 With one's head above water (6)
4 With goods as opposed to money (2,4)
9 Ancient Egyptian king (7)
10 Liquid measure (5)
11 Adjust again (5)
12 Fail to fulfil an obligation (7)
13 Maintain a firm position (4,3,4)
18 Forbear (7)
20 Terrible (5)
22 Shout with joy (5)
23 Cry out (7)
24 Australia's largest city (6)
25 Reached the height of one's powers (6)

DOWN

1 Unit of electrical current (6)
2 Gives for a limited time (5)
3 Changed for a particular purpose (7)
5 Man-made fibre (5)
6 Whole number (7)
7 Motor fuel (6)
8 Lacking sufficient staff (5-6)
14 Unburden (7)
15 Intended (7)
16 Goes on all fours (6)
17 Attribute responsibility to (6)
19 More than enough (5)
21 Haunch (5)

Solution see page 276

177

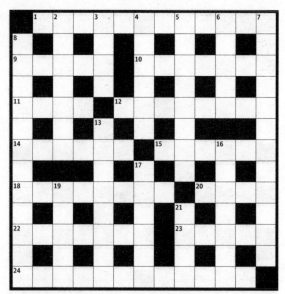

ACROSS

1 Source not to be cited (3,3,6)
9 Made a mistake (5)
10 Heavily walked upon (7)
11 Wigs? (4)
12 Dish of rice, fish and hard-boiled eggs (8)
14 Distinctive pattern of a Scottish clan (6)
15 Principles of right and wrong (6)
18 Capital of Bermuda (8)
20 East end of a church (4)
22 Insult (7)
23 Sexual liaison (5)
24 Psychiatrist (slang) (5,7)

DOWN

2 Collector of wild fungi, berries etc (7)
3 Receptacle for odds and ends (4)
4 Regard highly (6)
5 Extend (8)
6 Group living under a religious rule (5)
7 Yonks (7,5)
8 Intimate talk (5-2-5)
13 Device controlling inflow into a cistern (8)
16 Lacking reverence for God (7)
17 On the whole (6)
19 Muslim religious jurist (5)
21 Solid partition (4)

Solution see page 277

178

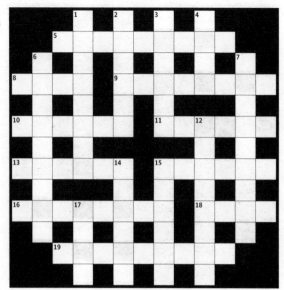

ACROSS

5 Upper figure in a fraction (9)
8 Comfortable — small secluded room (4)
9 31 Dec for the Scots (8)
10 Brighton & Hove, West Bromwich or Burton FC (6)
11 Large-rooted vegetable related to the cabbage (6)
13 Amount left over (6)
15 Pointy beard (6)
16 Sleepy guest at the Mad Hatter's tea party (8)
18 Large book (4)
19 Warlike (9)

DOWN

1 Bog (8)
2 Large female bird of the pheasant family (6)
3 Housefly larva (6)
4 Couch (4)
6 Change in a word's grammatical form — fix online (anag) (9)
7 Stuffing practice (9)
12 Try out how something works under realistic conditions (4,4)
14 In a way that shows excessive pride in oneself (6)
15 Hellenic Republic (6)
17 Very docile (4)

Solution see page 277

179

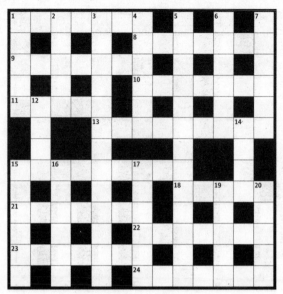

ACROSS

1 Lives (7)
8 Pretentiously exclusive (7)
9 Hold out (7)
10 Wear out (7)
11 Bush (5)
13 Never running out (9)
15 Bouncy (9)
18 Managed successfully (5)
21 Pernicious computer programs (7)
22 Itinerant (7)
23 Attendance (7)
24 Vocalists (7)

DOWN

1 Hawsers (5)
2 Search thoroughly (5)
3 Medical device for stabilising the heart (13)
4 Sheltering row of trees (6)
5 Batsman sent in to play out time late in the day (5,8)
6 District adjoining a town (6)
7 Evergreen shrub — try elm (anag) (6)
12 Artificially induced excitement (4)
14 Racing toboggan (4)
15 Distant — meteor (anag) (6)
16 Pay (6)
17 Happenings (6)
19 Army chaplain (5)
20 Harbour (5)

Solution see page 277

180

ACROSS

1 German wine — horse's back "ankle" (4)
3 Supports by putting in props (6,2)
9 Incentives (7)
10 Ship of the desert (5)
11 Far Eastern capital (5)
12 Oloroso or amontillado? (6)
14 Severe reprimand — laughing tones (anag) (6–7)
17 Final outcome (6)
19 Unleavened bread eaten at Passover (5)
22 Visit, as a ghost (5)
23 From Haifa, perhaps? (7)
24 Religious studies (8)
25 Don't go! (4)

DOWN

1 Falter (8)
2 Muscle spasm in the neck (5)
4 Making fine distinctions of little importance (4–9)
5 Explore with the aim of gaining useful information (5)
6 Caste of Japanese warriors (7)
7 Mush (4)
8 Number placement puzzle with a 9 x 9 grid (6)
13 Public dishonour (8)
15 Eighth rock from the Sun (7)
16 Melancholic (6)
18 Ritz or Hilton? (5)
20 Taking of another's property (5)
21 Natter (4)

Solution see page 277

181

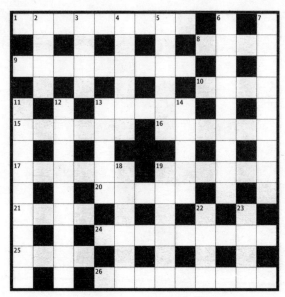

ACROSS

1 Cornish fishing village, flooded in 2004 — obstacles (anag) (9)
8 U2's star vocalist (4)
9 Large falcon (9)
10 Boxing contest (4)
13 Silent (5)
15 Break in continuity (6)
16 Highly seasoned stew (6)
17 Ethics (6)
19 Capital of Mozambique (6)
20 German semi-automatic pistol (5)
21 Italian "sparkler" (4)
24 Watched carefully (9)
25 Word such as "word" (4)
26 Motor racing over rough terrain (9)

DOWN

2 Bovine creatures (4)
3 Signals to actors (4)
4 Dog Star (6)
5 More extended (6)
6 Long solo speech (9)
7 Eager to be moving on (3,2,4)
11 French "sparkler" (9)
12 Indian Ocean island country (9)
13 Feather (5)
14 Devon–Cornwall boundary river (5)
18 Numbers puzzle (6)
19 Fine woollen yarn (6)
22 Impoverished (4)
23 Polynesian garlands (4)

Solution see page 278

182

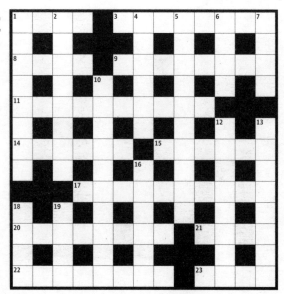

ACROSS

1 Collapse (4)
3 Overshadowed (8)
8 Open-air swimming pool (4)
9 Something transitory (8)
11 Occasion where everyone pays their share (5,5)
14 Light rowing boat (6)
15 Name of Roman emperor and only English pope (6)
17 Washing establishment (10)
20 Unfriendly (8)
21 Push out the lips alluringly (4)
22 In spite of what has happened (4,4)
23 Spell of duty (4)

DOWN

1 Collapse (4,4)
2 Curiosities (8)
4 Pickled flower buds used in sauces (6)
5 People from Reykjavik (10)
6 Hard white fat on sheep's kidneys (4)
7 Cart used for heavy loads (4)
10 Dispenser (10)
12 Musician of the highest technical skill (8)
13 Financier (8)
16 Dangerous (6)
18 Religious ceremony (4)
19 Line of people, one behind the other (4)

Solution see page 278

183

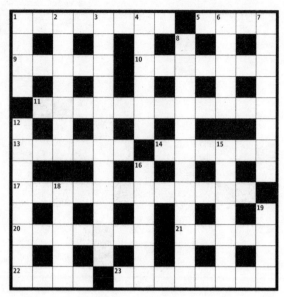

ACROSS

1 Treatment for feet and toenails (8)

5 Facts and figures (4)

9 Employee who runs errands (5)

10 Lancashire city (7)

11 1 November festival (3,6,3)

13 Helping (6)

14 Middle East country (6)

17 Expose oneself to unnecessary risk (4,4,4)

20 Coagulate (7)

21 Asian country (5)

22 Depose (4)

23 Continuous (8)

DOWN

1 Boy attendant (4)

2 Polluted (7)

3 What Miss Muffet ate (5,3,4)

4 Reimbursed (6)

6 Performed (5)

7 Vexatious (8)

8 Naval NCO (5,7)

12 Spanish vegetable soup, served cold (8)

15 Lifting device (7)

16 Taken unlawfully (6)

18 Female relatives (5)

19 Building for farm animals (4)

Solution see page 278

184

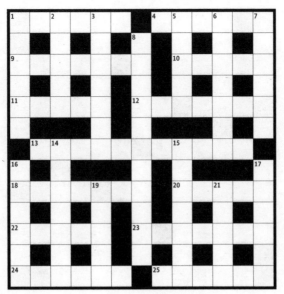

ACROSS

1 Despicable (6)

4 Dissertation (6)

9 Japanese code of chivalry (7)

10 Angry frown (5)

11 Air-filled cavity in one's head (5)

12 Pine leaves (7)

13 Deposit (4,7)

18 eg Carles Puigdemont (7)

20 Japanese cold rice dish (5)

22 Contagious viral disease (5)

23 Unnatural sounding and overformal (7)

24 Dead (2,4)

25 Cheap and nasty (6)

DOWN

1 Waylay (6)

2 Leader of the Argonauts (5)

3 Deep red (7)

5 Rushing (but with less speed?) (5)

6 Distended (7)

7 Big media display — belly-flop effect (6)

8 Rowan (8,3)

14 Very best (7)

15 Redeemer (7)

16 Shrewdness (6)

17 Noon (6)

19 Light amplification by stimulated emission of radiation (5)

21 Located (5)

Solution see page 278

185

ACROSS

1 Earlier (10)
7 Skinflint (7)
8 Bearing weapons (5)
10 Band worn round the waist (4)
11 Tincture of opium (8)
13 Counterfeiter (6)
15 Lacking material form (6)
17 Shy (8)
18 Great deal (4)
21 Sharpened with a stone (5)
22 In an opposing direction (7)
23 At this time (4,3,3)

DOWN

1 Fake (5)
2 Skin alive (4)
3 Member of the military police (6)
4 Billboard (8)
5 Candidate (7)
6 Et cetera (3,2,5)
9 Razed to the ground (10)
12 Be resentful of (8)
14 Cortège (7)
16 Hurting (2,4)
19 Sharp-tipped missile (5)
20 River running through Bath (4)

Solution see page 279

186

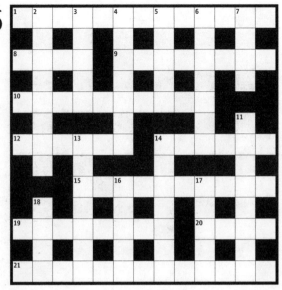

ACROSS

1 Pure guess (4,2,3,4)
8 Peak (4)
9 Unexpected fortune (8)
10 Author of The Pilgrim's Progress (4,6)
12 Spiteful (6)
14 Combat (6)
15 Dull — walker (10)
19 Don Quixote's region of Spain (2,6)
20 Finger feature (and tooth?) (4)
21 Swimming in one's birthday suit (6-7)

DOWN

2 Trance-inducing (8)
3 Poison (5)
4 North Cornish seaside resort (7)
5 Useful (5)
6 Extinct (7)
7 Little stream (4)
11 German shepherd (8)
13 Skipper (7)
14 Type of rice (7)
16 Lure (5)
17 Preliminary period (3-2)
18 Old torture instrument (4)

Solution see page 279

187

ACROSS

1 Halt (4,2,4)
7 Children's game (7)
8 Ground covered by a mat of grass and grass roots (5)
10 Deposit of valuable ore running through other rocks (4)
11 Serving to commemorate the dead (8)
13 One of seven centres of spiritual power in the human body (6)
15 Causing irritation (6)
17 Prosperous (8)
18 Repair by sewing (4)
21 UK shipping forecast area (5)
22 Progressive — open-handed (7)
23 Over a short distance (5,5)

DOWN

1 Remedied (5)
2 Backless slipper (4)
3 Sample intended to stimulate interest (6)
4 One who renovates works of art (8)
5 Language widely used in East Africa (7)
6 Shown to be a party to (10)
9 With meticulous care (10)
12 Book of the Bible (8)
14 Entrance (7)
16 Fisherman (6)
19 Go well together (5)
20 Port and holiday centre on the west coast of Scotland (4)

Solution see page 279

188

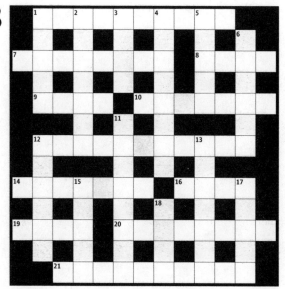

ACROSS

1 Tackle a task with determination (6,4)
7 Horticulturist (8)
8 Wet thoroughly (4)
9 Lofty (4)
10 Green gem (7)
12 Specialist in the use of X-rays (11)
14 Bouts of illness (7)
16 Supplied with footwear (4)
19 Tofu source (4)
20 Bend over (with laughter or pain?) (6,2)
21 A very long time ago (3,4,3)

DOWN

1 Brute (5)
2 Cosseted (7)
3 Wild cat — text browser (4)
4 Setting for The Hound of the Baskervilles (8)
5 More judicious (5)
6 Nureyev's forte (6)
11 Mundane (8)
12 Fixed allotment (6)
13 Breathed in (7)
15 Embarrass (5)
17 Question (5)
18 Russian parliament (4)

Solution see page 279

189

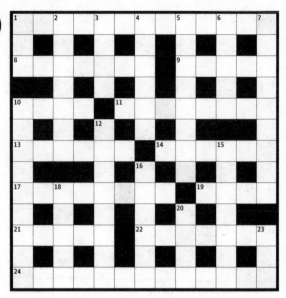

ACROSS

1 Fellow soldier (7-2-4)
8 Hereditary knight (7)
9 Book for someone swearing? (5)
10 Chain armour (4)
11 Sheets and pillowcases (8)
13 Nakedness (6)
14 Counter-factual (6)
17 Leading (8)
19 Feeble (4)
21 Heraldic black (5)
22 Knoll (7)
24 Ostensibly (2,3,4,2,2)

DOWN

1 Hazelnut (3)
2 Not single (7)
3 Stuart queen (4)
4 Word indicating the following alternatives (6)
5 Taking small bites (8)
6 Christmas card bird (5)
7 Author of The Grapes of Wrath (9)
10 Pre-election policy declaration (9)
12 Disorderly rush (8)
15 Utter fluently (4,3)
16 Volcanic island near Naples (6)
18 Automaton (5)
20 Unrestrained joy (4)
23 Equipment (3)

Solution see page 280

190

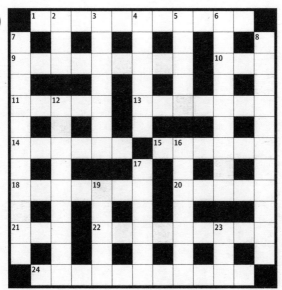

ACROSS

1 Adapt to a new environment (11)
9 Mischievous fairy (9)
10 Scottish mountain (3)
11 Plunder (5)
13 Mythical horse/man (7)
14 Noisy, lavish party (6)
15 Diverse (6)
18 Foul-smelling (7)
20 Incantation (5)
21 Wrong (3)
22 Grass (9)
24 Likely winner (5,6)

DOWN

2 Male swan (3)
3 Unties (7)
4 Ill will (6)
5 Projection used in a mortise joint (5)
6 Underwater (9)
7 Physiological need to drink — resists hint (anag) (11)
8 Disbelief (11)
12 Alien (9)
16 Contestant losing by a large margin (4-3)
17 Young cow (6)
19 Constellation on the celestial equator — giant hunter of Greek mythology (5)
23 Intoxicating drink (3)

Solution see page 280

191

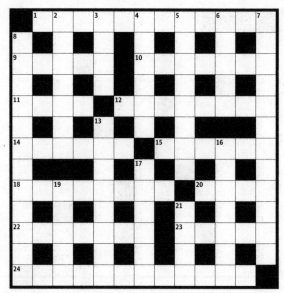

ACROSS

1 Result of exports exceeding imports (5,7)
9 Uninspired writers (5)
10 Naturally grown (7)
11 Female servant (4)
12 Surrounded closely (6,2)
14 Worthless (2-4)
15 Be adamant (6)
18 Better (8)
20 Small seabird with a forked tail (4)
22 Sums (7)
23 Make progress (3,2)
24 Talent for talking (4,2,3,3)

DOWN

2 Moving back and forth (7)
3 Time of day after sunset (4)
4 Tobacco user (6)
5 The Grenadier Guards, for example (8)
6 Furrowed (5)
7 Best (6,2,4)
8 Daisy roots, china plate and dicky bird, for example (7,5)
13 Resort on the Bay of Naples (8)
16 Reluctance to move (7)
17 English county — sorted (anag) (6)
19 Draft copy of printed text (5)
21 Monstrous giant (4)

Solution see page 280

192

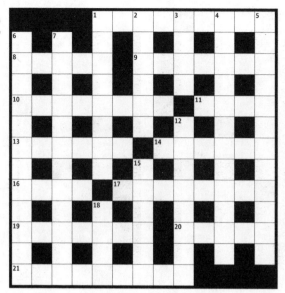

ACROSS

1 Bed, breakfast and one main meal (4,5)
8 Terms of reference (5)
9 Grants immunity to (7)
10 Upset (by a stirrer?) (8)
11 Chessman (4)
13 Breeding ground (6)
14 See pal (anag) — charm (6)
16 Book of the Old Testament (4)
17 Living thing — man's giro (anag) (8)
19 The shakes (7)
20 Body of established rules or principles (5)
21 Cleanser (9)

DOWN

1 Milliner (8)
2 Look suggestively (6)
3 A pot of tea? (4)
4 Computer programs (12)
5 Difference of opinion (12)
6 Checked for drink-driving (6-6)
7 Grudge (12)
12 Sharply defined (5-3)
15 Daniel Defoe's castaway (6)
18 Coarse, ill-mannered person (4)

Solution see page 280

193

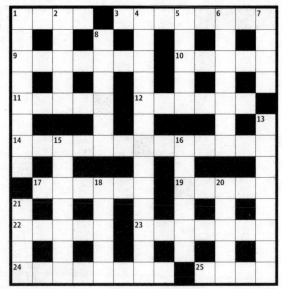

ACROSS

1 Conduit for a fluid (4)
3 Stiff(ened) (8)
9 One who hesitates fearfully (7)
10 Dressing served with food (5)
11 Fabric (originally from New York and London) (5)
12 Legislative assembly (6)
14 Opposition frontbenchers (6,7)
17 Woody tropical grass (6)
19 Royal (5)
22 Unsoiled (5)
23 Apparent (7)
24 So-so (8)
25 Male protagonist (4)

DOWN

1 Moisture from the air at night — new sides (anag) (8)
2 Polite (5)
4 Relating to dancing (13)
5 Gone up (5)
6 Texas city (7)
7 Source of venison (4)
8 Promptly (6)
13 Long dagger (8)
15 Finished (2,2,3)
16 European capital (6)
18 Hackneyed (5)
20 Birds in a gaggle (5)
21 Fraudulent scheme (4)

Solution see page 281

194

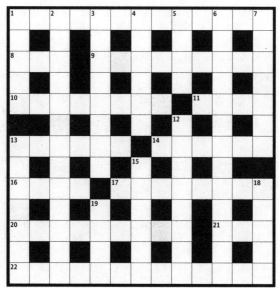

ACROSS

1 Liable to mishaps (8-5)
8 Military manoeuvres (abbr) (3)
9 Blood cell (9)
10 Disappear gradually (4,4)
11 System of religious beliefs and rituals (4)
13 Sign of the zodiac (6)
14 Last Anglo-Saxon king of England (6)
16 That's a relief! (4)
17 Planes (8)
20 Adherents (9)
21 Irritate (3)
22 Avian messenger (7,6)

DOWN

1 Stand-offish (5)
2 ATM (4,9)
3 No longer living (8)
4 Land of fjords (6)
5 Publicise — stop (4)
6 How to start off a children's story? (4,4,1,4)
7 Put up (7)
12 Spring-flowering plants (8)
13 Nickname of Haitian dictator François Duvalier (4,3)
15 Steering device — ploughman (6)
18 Symbol (5)
19 Iconic economy car (introduced in 1959) (4)

Solution see page 281

195

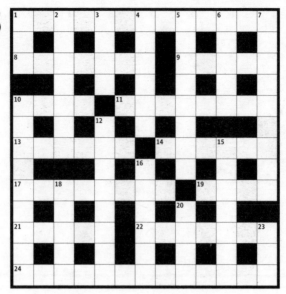

ACROSS

1 Have great or unexpected success (3,3,7)
8 Ancient writing material (7)
9 Evergreen tree (5)
10 Herb of the parsley family (4)
11 White Cliffs of Dover singer, b. 1917 (4,4)
13 Groove (6)
14 Mediterranean principality (6)
17 Radioactive element (8)
19 Yonks (4)
21 Slow lazy accent (5)
22 High-handedness (7)
24 Finished (4,3,6)

DOWN

1 Informal dance (3)
2 Drinker (7)
3 Listen! (4)
4 Semi-precious quartz stone — boy's name (6)
5 Crested parrot (8)
6 Field where rice is grown (5)
7 Despotic (9)
10 Swindled (9)
12 Caroline (anag) — girl's name (8)
15 Grow — intensify (7)
16 Caused to be quiet (6)
18 Retinue (5)
20 Recognised leader in some field (4)
23 Slender stick (3)

Solution see page 281

196

ACROSS

1 Spectacles (7)
8 Smarty-pants (4-3)
9 Bilk (7)
10 Diver's garment (7)
11 Band with Liam and Noel Gallagher (5)
13 Continue despite difficulties (9)
15 One standing for office (9)
18 Cultivated land (5)
21 Small detail (7)
22 Bounce back (7)
23 Aerial (7)
24 Founder-hero of Athens (7)

DOWN

1 Enthusiastic enjoyment (5)
2 Au revoir, amigo! (5)
3 Extremely funny (4-9)
4 Impale (6)
5 Swede, for example (4,9)
6 Fully developed (6)
7 Cheerful and carefree (6)
12 North Indian city, former capital of the Mogul empire (4)
14 Breather (4)
15 Fight against (6)
16 XC (6)
17 Volcanic mount in eastern Turkey (6)
19 Wingless bloodsucker (5)
20 Conceals (5)

Solution see page 281

197

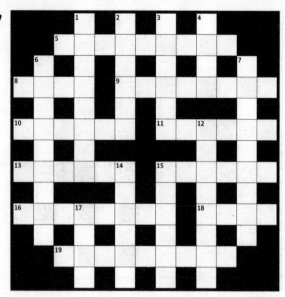

ACROSS

5 True — real (9)
8 Seducer — gobble down (4)
9 Ship — glass (8)
10 Wrinkle (6)
11 Elastic substance — unit of play (at bridge) (6)
13 Join the other side (6)
15 Large green vegetable (6)
16 City of central Scotland, "Gateway to the Highlands" (8)
18 British nobleman (4)
19 Lewd (9)

DOWN

1 Attractive muscular men (8)
2 Bodily matter (6)
3 Fairly (6)
4 Besides (4)
6 Small green vegetable (9)
7 Bugbear (4,5)
12 Cook on an open fire (8)
14 Chinese island (6)
15 Bird — obsessive collector (6)
17 Harvest (4)

Solution see page 282

198

ACROSS

1 Withdraw in the face of opposition (4,4)
5 Engage (4)
9 Respiratory organs (5)
10 Endanger (7)
11 Participant in a public protest (12)
13 Port — stoned (anag) (6)
14 Craving for drink (6)
17 Deliberate pretence — exaggerated display (12)
20 Not strict (7)
21 Not happy (5)
22 Not interesting (4)
23 Tiny organisms drifting in the sea (8)

DOWN

1 Great size (4)
2 Setting (7)
3 Not joined (12)
4 Playfully quaint behaviour (6)
6 Greet (anag) — wading bird (5)
7 Amusement (8)
8 Arrest — dread (12)
12 Doubtful — suspect (2–6)
15 Begin anew (7)
16 High-protein pulse (6)
18 Not to be altered (5)
19 Not fat (4)

Solution see page 282

199

ACROSS

1 Decapitate (6)
4 Idiosyncrasy (5)
7 Cake-burning king (6)
8 Distinctive flag (6)
9 Game with 18 holes (4)
10 I must think about this (3,2,3)
12 Automatic rifle first produced in the Soviet Union in 1949 (11)
17 Riding event (8)
19 Something typical (4)
20 Approximately (6)
21 Fervour (6)
22 Invited (5)
23 (Of food) served in alcohol and set alight (6)

DOWN

1 Steer (7)
2 Injurious (7)
3 Region of southern Spain (9)
4 Misgiving (5)
5 French dramatist, leading figure in the theatre of the absurd, d. 1994 (7)
6 Nucleus (6)
11 In vain (2,2,5)
13 Wrestling hold (7)
14 What Richard III would have given for a horse (7)
15 Greenery (7)
16 Arboreal lizard (6)
18 Perfected (5)

Solution see page 282

200

ACROSS

1 Green shoots, cooked and eaten as a vegetable (9)

8 1960s' style of abstract painting, with dramatic visual effects (2,3)

9 With a legally valid will (7)

10 Annual circle in a trunk showing its age (4,4)

11 Make more acute (4)

13 Drinking glass (6)

14 Hello! (6)

16 Sieve (4)

17 Conforming to established standard (8)

19 Edible marine mollusc — Oban ale (anag) (7)

20 Extra time in bed in the morning (3-2)

21 North Korean capital (9)

DOWN

1 Person appointed to act for another in legal or business matters (8)

2 Obvious (6)

3 Reddish-brown coating caused by oxidation (4)

4 Book with a comic strip format (7,5)

5 Trying to persuade by flattery (5-7)

6 Token stuck on a letter — ATM stoppages (anag) (7,5)

7 Large Asian beast domesticated for use as a draught animal (5,7)

12 Long and exhausting march (8)

15 Old Spanish coin (6)

18 Smell unpleasantly (4)

Solution see page 282

201

ACROSS

1 Beat about the bush (10)
7 Capital of Ontario (7)
8 European capital — Trojan prince (5)
10 Fastened (4)
11 Joni ___ , Canadian singer-songwriter, b. 1943 (8)
13 Happens (6)
15 Butt of a comedian's jokes (6)
17 In fact (8)
18 Avian symbols of wisdom (4)
21 Talks incessantly (5)
22 Gland in the neck (7)
23 "Uncertainty principle" mathematical physicist, d. 1976 — begins here (anag) (10)

DOWN

1 Strange and disturbing (5)
2 Vases (4)
3 Menuhin's instrument (6)
4 Maximum amount that can be contained (8)
5 Underwater projectile (7)
6 Still (10)
9 Cut of beef (10)
12 Little Rock's state (8)
14 Dead skin on a fingernail (7)
16 Famous Five author, d. 1968 (6)
19 Incorrect (5)
20 Kind (4)

Solution see page 283

202

ACROSS

1 Old-fashioned and conservative (5-5)
7 Most desirable (7)
8 Unfledged pigeon (5)
10 Not a sausage (4)
11 Thin unleavened pancake (8)
13 Without difficulty (6)
15 Heedless (6)
17 Freshwater turtle (8)
18 Sweet variety of tangelo from Jamaica (4)
21 Fragrance (5)
22 From the UK (7)
23 Not touched by a blue pencil? (10)

DOWN

1 Unsprung roll-up mattress (5)
2 Unable to speak (4)
3 Colour of ripe lemons (6)
4 Discompose (8)
5 Close-fitting padded jacket of Tudor and Stuart England (7)
6 House plant, popular at Christmas — tiniest OAP (anag) (10)
9 Device that signals when a car is slowing (5,5)
12 Bust split (8)
14 Quality cut of beef (7)
16 Rain cloud (6)
19 Suggestive dance — reduce to fine particles (5)
20 Fashion designer Christian, famous for his 1947 New Look (4)

Solution see page 283

203

ACROSS

1 Modest (6)
4 Grieves (6)
8 Evil spirit (5)
9 Kitchen utensil (7)
10 Picks (7)
11 Stressful (5)
12 Achiever (4-5)
17 Brown in front of a fire (5)
19 Greenery (7)
21 Small strongly-flavoured food fish (7)
22 Scandinavian — vegetable (5)
23 Everything one owns (6)
24 Robber (6)

DOWN

1 Work out (6)
2 Gigantic — extinct animal (7)
3 Encircles (5)
5 Obviously (7)
6 French sculptor of The Kiss, d. 1917 (5)
7 Water ice (6)
9 In a shy and timid manner (9)
13 Clear off! (3,4)
14 Run into another vehicle from behind (4-3)
15 Relaxed (2,4)
16 Discover (6)
18 Racecourse near Windsor (5)
20 Bewildered (2,3)

Solution see page 283

204

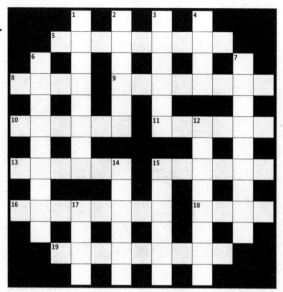

ACROSS

5 Entertainment based on broad and earthy humour (9)

8 Branch of a tree (risky to go out on) (4)

9 Take fraudulently (8)

10 Chesty (anag) — reaping tool (6)

11 Payment for services rendered (6)

13 Italian archbishop of Canterbury,

10 1093–1109 (6)

15 Internet search engine (6)

16 Having another other half! (8)

18 Price (4)

19 French-style restaurant (9)

DOWN

1 Expose one's body in hot weather (8)

2 Part of garment covering the arm (6)

3 Line showing points of equal barometric pressure (6)

4 Sound of a bumblebee (4)

6 US state bordering on Lakes Superior and Michigan (9)

7 Cleric who holds more than one benefice at a time — April lust (anag) (9)

12 Kind of wallpaper with grainy surface texture (8)

14 Follower of the Chinese Chairman's Little Red Book — Taoism (anag) (6)

15 Oil well not in need of a pump (6)

17 Distinctive but intangible quality (4)

Solution see page 283

205

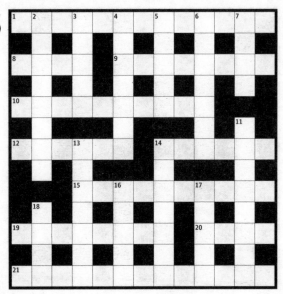

ACROSS

1 Insurgent — involving dramatic change (13)

8 Blow-up mattress (4)

9 Deceptive (8)

10 Royal Troon or Carnoustie, for example (4,6)

12 TV show intended to be humorous (6)

14 Statistic — physique (6)

15 Assumed name (3,2,5)

19 Relating to the home (8)

20 Egyptian canal (4)

21 Soft cleaner (7,6)

DOWN

2 Divided into tenuously related parts (8)

3 Discontinuous (2–3)

4 Constant (7)

5 Lazybones (5)

6 Sum of money put by as a reserve (4,3)

7 Not well done! (4)

11 First performance (8)

13 Satisfied — subject matter (7)

14 Taken to the cleaners (7)

16 Liturgical headdress (5)

17 Tables (5)

18 Flower — climbed (4)

Solution see page 284

206

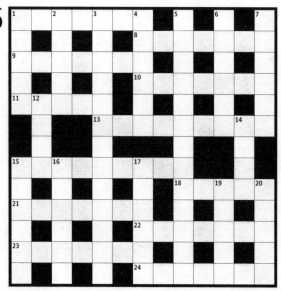

ACROSS

1 Philistine giant slain by David (7)
8 Self-inflicted harm (3,4)
9 Give assistance in time of difficulty (7)
10 Haranguing — horizontal bar on supports (7)
11 Histrionic incident (5)
13 Sweet smell — clone deer (anag) (9)
15 Approach slowly and imperceptibly (5,2,2)
18 Triangular part of a wall supporting a ridged roof (5)
21 Nocturnal raptor (4,3)
22 Mediocre (7)
23 Element used in electronic circuits (7)
24 Exhibition (7)

DOWN

1 Draws breath sharply (5)
2 Filthy money? (5)
3 Beyond criticism (5,8)
4 Repellent (6)
5 Reluctance (13)
6 Healing drink (6)
7 Deadly epidemic (6)
12 Mrs Mopp (4)
14 Fossil fuel (4)
15 Art movement pioneered by Braque and Picasso before 1914 (6)
16 Signs on (6)
17 Country that joined the European Union in 2004 (6)
19 Rowdy scuffle (5)
20 Foe (5)

Solution see page 284

207

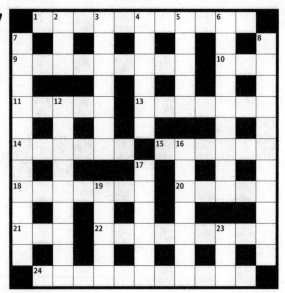

ACROSS

1 Unintentional confusion of one word with another (by someone in a Sheridan play?) (11)
9 Petty finder of errors (3-6)
10 Personal pride (3)
11 Gulf of Naples island (5)
13 Cherry-red (7)
14 Foam (6)
15 Vicious (6)
18 Very dry spell (7)
20 Measuring device (5)
21 State of armed struggle (3)
22 Mention (9)
24 Camera device — see fly shine (anag) (7,4)

DOWN

2 Toward's a ship's stern (3)
3 Stupid (7)
4 Jaunty (6)
5 Anorak (5)
6 Sense something is amiss (5,1,3)
7 Apply oneself seriously (7,4)
8 Compassionate (4-7)
12 Medley (9)
16 Unscrupulous (7)
17 Pompous (6)
19 Personal circumference (5)
23 Gran (3)

Solution see page 284

208

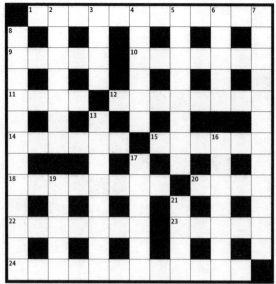

ACROSS

1 South African city (12)
9 Eminent (5)
10 Wool fat (7)
11 Gasp for breath (like a hot dog?) (4)
12 Forebear (8)
14 Movie role for several dog stars (6)
15 Teaching establishment (6)
18 At a hedge (anag) — make progress (3,5)
20 Flock of larks, quails or swans (4)
22 Moment for a light afternoon meal? (7)
23 Show with broncobusters (5)
24 Results — parlour game (12)

DOWN

2 Excursions (7)
3 Verdi opera (4)
4 Stockings (6)
5 Term of imprisonment (8)
6 Dark (5)
7 Angels yonder (anag) — governing body of the Church of England (7,5)
8 Not expressing regret (12)
13 Building with many storeys (4-4)
16 Expected before now (7)
17 Something French for 22? (6)
19 Two (5)
21 Cereal fibre (4)

Solution see page 284

209

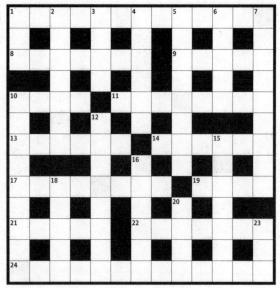

ACROSS

1 Unexpectedly behaves in very helpful way (5,2,6)

8 Glowing (7)

9 Believer in the existence of God (5)

10 Bankrupt (4)

11 Merchant ships with a limited range of operation (8)

13 Suppress anything considered obscene or politically unacceptable (6)

14 Place of worship (6)

17 Died (6,2)

19 Arab marketplace (4)

21 Rummage (5)

22 Foodstuffs (7)

24 Can't remember what to say next (4,3,6)

DOWN

1 Vehicle (3)

2 United States president — Wisconsin's capital (7)

3 Glance over (4)

4 Go on one's rounds (6)

5 Salad vegetables (8)

6 Indian corn (5)

7 As it were (2,2,5)

10 Reverse a previous strong view (4–5)

12 Intelligible (8)

15 Put forward a plan (7)

16 Foreign stock exchange (6)

18 They're always under one's feet! (5)

20 Irritation of the skin (4)

23 Turf (3)

Solution see page 285

210

ACROSS

1 Old Testament book of sacred songs (6)

4 Boring documents and written information (5)

7 Very little to eat — goodness gracious me! (6)

8 Substance that alchemists believed could turn base metals into gold (6)

9 Remedy (4)

10 Female rubber? (8)

12 Colour — to be gentler (anag) (6,5)

17 Household servant (often faithful and old!) (8)

19 Urban area larger than a village (4)

20 Young rascal — horror (6)

21 Wildcat — loo etc (anag) (6)

22 Mawkish (5)

23 Distinctive characteristic (6)

DOWN

1 Unsettle (7)

2 Support attached to the side of a chair (7)

3 Monk's mule (anag) — eg honeydew (4,5)

4 Lamps — daffodils (5)

5 Melange (7)

6 Messenger of the gods (6)

11 Make something distasteful seem more palatable? (5-4)

13 Part of a rock formation above the surface (7)

14 Drastic — limit (7)

15 Big Apple (3,4)

16 On the house (6)

18 Creamy white (5)

Solution see page 285

211

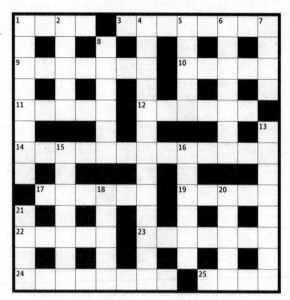

ACROSS

1 Wine buyer's basic quantity (4)
3 Climbing plant with fragrant flowers (5,3)
9 Gin, vodka, rum etc (7)
10 Choice piece of loin steak (1–4)
11 Cricketing position (3–2)
12 Period of decline (6)
14 Utterly — radically (4,3,6)
17 Poles used for walking high above the ground (6)
19 British film and television award (5)
22 Cutting down (5)
23 Transgression (7)
24 Target's centre (8)
25 Conspire (4)

DOWN

1 Fine soft wool (8)
2 Spotted (5)
4 1957 musical set in New York City (4,4,5)
5 Consumed (5)
6 Dietary requirement (7)
7 Elderly (4)
8 Adult home of Beethoven, Brahms, Mozart and Schubert (6)
13 Of the poorest quality (8)
15 Being tested (2,5)
16 Be transferred by contact or association (3,3)
18 Former capital of Nigeria (5)
20 Last (5)
21 Raiment (4)

Solution see page 285

212

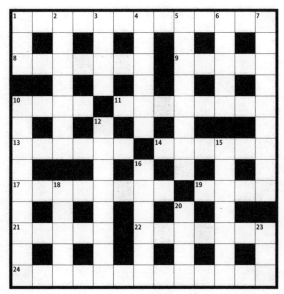

ACROSS

1 Shakespeare play (5,2,6)
8 Worried (7)
9 Din (5)
10 Doctrines (4)
11 Matter sinking to the bottom of a liquid (8)
13 A high-level meeting? (6)
14 Angry stare (6)
17 Precise (8)
19 Power distribution network (4)
21 Excite (5)
22 Capital of the Isle of Man (7)
24 Polychromatic (13)

DOWN

1 Plantation product (3)
2 Greatest possible quantity (7)
3 Inert gas (4)
4 Didn't eat (6)
5 Able to be felt (8)
6 Select group (5)
7 Shielded (9)
10 Photo-sharing app (9)
12 Victorian prime minister (8)
15 Songbird (7)
16 Artist's workroom (6)
18 Rude and mean-spirited fellow (5)
20 Wife of Jupiter (4)
23 Unhappy (3)

Solution see page 285

213

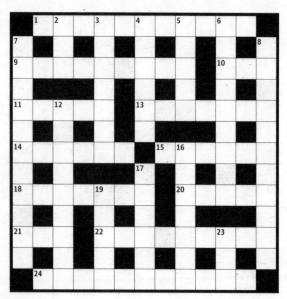

ACROSS

1 Ruthlessly (2,4,5)
9 Radical (9)
10 Fish (3)
11 Wrinkled (5)
13 Place of total privacy (7)
14 Acquired through effort (6)
15 Cultivator that breaks up the soil (6)
18 Useless person (2-5)
20 Cringe in fear (5)
21 Meshwork (3)
22 Tolerate — endure (3,2,4)
24 Thumb tacks (to Americans) (7,4)

DOWN

2 Mechanical fastener (3)
3 Late (7)
4 Most arid (6)
5 Spill the beans (3,2)
6 Depose (9)
7 Having good, if ill-advised, intentions (4-7)
8 Culpable (11)
12 Polaris (5,4)
16 Intoxicating beverage tasting like a soft drink (7)
17 Of a Greek island, centre of the Minoan civilisation (6)
19 Custard apple (5)
23 Tavern (3)

Solution see page 286

ACROSS

1 Ranting public speaker (3-7)
7 A little piece at a time (3,2,3)
8 Circular tent (4)
9 Sharp taste (4)
10 Study of the structure of animals (7)
12 Pale yellow vegetable fat used to make chocolate — true tobacco (anag) (5,6)
14 Wimp (7)
16 Prayer ending (4)
19 Mixture of fat and flour used as basis for sauces (4)
20 American whose first language is Spanish (8)
21 Attractive young spouse of an affluent older man (6,4)

DOWN

1 Unexpected development (5)
2 Strain of plague (7)
3 American vagrant (4)
4 Disposed to be disloyal (8)
5 Land of the pharaohs (5)
6 Shake (6)
11 Cut of meat (4,4)
12 Chemical element found in coal (6)
13 Drums (7)
15 Pugilistic dog? (5)
17 Dissonant sound (5)
18 Observe (4)

Solution see page 286

215

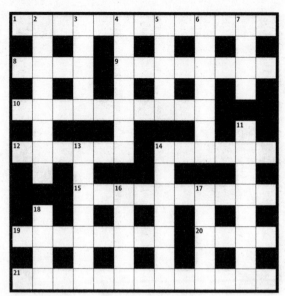

ACROSS

1 Resort in desperation to inadequate remedy (5,2,6)

8 One of two bones of the forearm (4)

9 Prime minister's official country residence (8)

10 Large wine bottle — biblical patriarch (10)

12 Wise counsellor (6)

14 Destitution (6)

15 Violating accepted standards or rules (10)

19 Supply with water (8)

20 Versifier (4)

21 As a whole (2,3,8)

DOWN

2 Freed from anxiety (8)

3 Shatter violently (5)

4 One imputing guilt (7)

5 Trance (5)

6 Abrade (7)

7 Slender but strong and agile (4)

11 Most majestic (8)

13 Person travelling for pleasure (7)

14 Shield from danger (7)

16 Sudden forceful flow (5)

17 Thin out — spill (5)

18 Small active brown northern hemisphere bird (4)

Solution see page 286

216

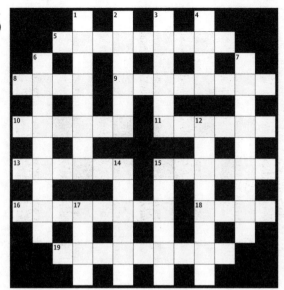

ACROSS

5 Proceed without the help of others (2,2,5)

8 Comms code for G (4)

9 Done (8)

10 Profundities (6)

11 Cease operating (3,3)

13 Extravagant (6)

15 Truthful (6)

16 Eating to excess (8)

18 Cupid, son of Aphrodite (4)

19 Having taken everything into consideration (2,7)

DOWN

1 Small pieces of coloured paper (8)

2 English county (abbr) (6)

3 Medical centre (6)

4 Responsibility (4)

6 Olympic field event (4,5)

7 Feeling of intense disgust (9)

12 Predisposition (8)

14 Oriental tobacco pipe with a long tube (6)

15 Period of one's greatest productivity (6)

17 Portable shelter (4)

Solution see page 286

217

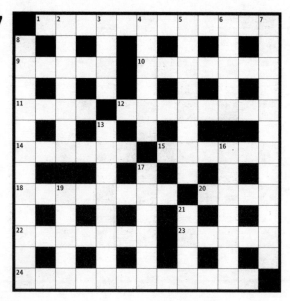

ACROSS

1 Attain recognition (4,4,4)
9 Off-the-cuff remark (2-3)
10 North American bison (7)
11 Stylish enthusiasm (4)
12 Veteran, one expected to 7 (3,5)
14 Abhorrence (6)
15 Military greeting (6)
18 Predator (8)
20 Therefore (4)
22 Divorce (5,2)
23 Without others being involved (5)
24 Failure to act with prudence (12)

DOWN

2 Eat salt (anag) — if nothing else (2,5)
3 Island of Napoleon's first exile (4)
4 Of marriageable age (6)
5 Use persuasive flattery (4-4)
6 Old saying (5)
7 Understand normal procedures (4,3,5)
8 Confront the consequences of one's actions (4,3,5)
13 Confutation (8)
16 Displaces — or put so (anag) (7)
17 Lures (6)
19 Potentate (5)
21 Futile (4)

Solution see page 287

218

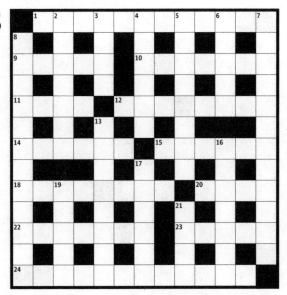

ACROSS

1 Arm of the Atlantic to the south of the United States (4,2,6)

9 Alphabetical list of a book's contents (5)

10 Fix firmly (7)

11 Rank immediately above viscount (4)

12 California city (3,5)

14 Waterproof jacket (6)

15 A 19 player (6)

18 Indonesian islander (8)

20 Instruction to cancel a deletion (4)

22 One with privileged information (7)

23 Short poem with a song-like quality (5)

24 Computing jargon (12)

DOWN

2 Experience (7)

3 Sly — sexy (4)

4 Day for eating fish? (6)

5 Hasten (8)

6 Fatuous (5)

7 Correction of dental irregularities (12)

8 Over-the-shoulder carrying technique (8,4)

13 Extinct elephant ancestor (8)

16 Withdrawal from a position (7)

17 Croatian capital (6)

19 Sounds produced by musical instruments (5)

21 Divulge secret information (4)

Solution see page 287

219

ACROSS

1 Tree feller (10)
7 Fielding position (4,3)
8 Merriment (5)
10 Baby food (4)
11 Inability to sleep (8)
13 Anaesthetised (6)
15 Come to rest — North Yorkshire market town (6)
17 Imperil (8)
18 Tools for punching holes (4)
21 Baking agent (5)
22 First man in space (7)
23 Unnecessarily (10)

DOWN

1 Connections (5)
2 Clement — type of beer (4)
3 Motor (6)
4 Large plane (5,3)
5 Small crown (7)
6 Audacity (10)
9 Opportune (6-4)
12 Brought together again (8)
14 Act as go-between (7)
16 Horse (slang) (3-3)
19 Verbose (5)
20 Donkey's years (4)

Solution see page 287

220

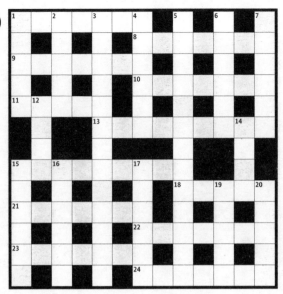

ACROSS

1 Categories (7)

8 One of Christ's 12 original disciples (7)

9 Engine holding the world speed record for a steam locomotive, set at 123mph in 1938 (7)

10 Widened (7)

11 Vault beneath a church (5)

13 In haste (9)

15 Roomy (9)

18 Motorcyclist (5)

21 Out of the ordinary (7)

22 Disregarded (7)

23 Relative by marriage (7)

24 Important energy distributor — Ian's mag (anag) (3,4)

DOWN

1 Humorous (5)

2 Eg brass or bronze (5)

3 Endure to the end (4,3,6)

4 Unhappier (6)

5 Insurance premium reduction (2-6,5)

6 Declared (6)

7 Lethal (6)

12 Flightless bird — satellite of Saturn (4)

14 Solitary (4)

15 Maladroit (6)

16 Dried plums (6)

17 Looking lecherously (6)

19 Fate — destiny (5)

20 Radioactive gas (5)

Solution see page 287

221

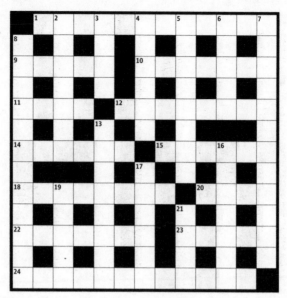

ACROSS

1,15 Canada's smallest province (6,6,6)
9 Path of one celestial body about another (5)
10 Upstart (7)
11 Become immoveable (4)
12 Cosy — loose (8)
14 Instrument used for a fight (6)
15 See 1
18 Vessels used to deepen channels (8)
20 Metal, Zn (4)
22 Small fish (7)
23 Espresso added to frothed steamed milk (5)
24 What one needs to get on (8,4)

DOWN

2 Mother of Jacob and Esau (7)
3 Distinction (4)
4 Swell (6)
5 Rodent that sleeps most of the day (8)
6 Elite group (1-4)
7 Routemaster, for example (6-6)
8 www (5,4,3)
13 Lark, for example (8)
16 Woman in a flying machine (7)
17 Fire-breather (6)
19 Juan Perón's wife (5)
21 Alliance of countries (4)

Solution see page 288

222

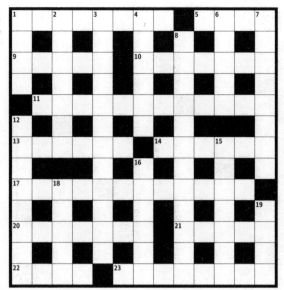

ACROSS

1 Dejected (8)
5 Principal (4)
9 Criminal (5)
10 Gradual decline (7)
11 Financial statement (7,5)
13 Impudent (6)
14 Long-haired sheepdog (6)
17 London borough — Matthew's role (anag) (5,7)
20 Undecided (2,5)
21 Itinerary (5)
22 Steeped in blood (4)
23 Ship's crew's living quarters (4,4)

DOWN

1 Useless — broken (4)
2 Social security (7)
3 Irascible (12)
4 Oration (6)
6 Not yet pushing up the daisies (5)
7 A prime number (8)
8 Upper chamber of Parliament (5,2,5)
12 Witheringly scornful (8)
15 Part of a BLT (7)
16 Material for making fences, roofing etc — Australian acacia (6)
18 Long-legged shore bird (5)
19 Magistrate — schoolmaster (old slang) (4)

Solution see page 288

223

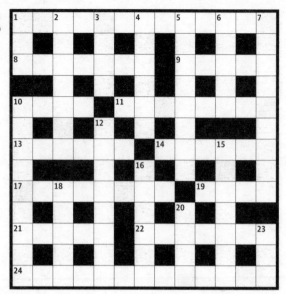

ACROSS

1 A poor catcher (13)
8 Military commander (7)
9 Sign of the zodiac (5)
10 Females in the flock (4)
11 Enlisted — sort of writing? (6,2)
13 London rail terminus (6)
14 Church caretaker (6)
17 Observing (8)
19 Spot (4)
21 Interior (5)
22 Not cognisant (7)
24 Gloucestershire market town on the Fosse Way (4-2-3-4)

DOWN

1 Secret listening device (3)
2 Underground passages (7)
3 Acquire through merit (4)
4 Go after (6)
5 Not any more (2,6)
6 Receded (5)
7 Do for blokes (4,5)
10 Alpine plant, celebrated in song (9)
12 Womaniser (8)
15 Geheime Staatspolizei (7)
16 Inequitable (6)
18 Latin-American dance (5)
20 Titled lady (4)
23 Final stage (3)

Solution see page 288

224

ACROSS

1 Small change to achieve a desired result (10)

7 Women's hat maker (8)

8 Repast (4)

9 Front part of the leg above the ankle (4)

10 Computer operating system with a graphical user interface (7)

12 Delighted interest (11)

14 Hung (7)

16 Street of houses formerly used as stables (4)

19 Subdued — spineless (4)

20 Open to suggestion (8)

21 Formed into a whole (10)

DOWN

1 First sign of the zodiac (5)

2 Celebratory parties (7)

3 Sound in mind (4)

4 Borderline (8)

5 Member of a wandering pastoral community (5)

6 Author of On the Origin of Species, d. 1882 (6)

11 Free (8)

12 Large container for serving drink (6)

13 Approximate (7)

15 Hit it off (3,2)

17 Cold dish of vegetables (5)

18 Grazing animal(s) (4)

Solution see page 288

SOLUTIONS

1

2

3

4

SOLUTIONS

5

C	E	R	E	A	L		S	P	I	R	I	T
A		O		L		H		O		E		W
S	E	V	I	L	L	E		P	A	T	I	O
L		E		A		A		E		W		W
L	O	R	R	Y		V	I	S	C	E	R	A
E		E			E		E		E		Y
	G	A	R	D	E	N	P	A	R	T	Y	
A		N		K		L		N			N
G	E	T	E	V	E	N		S	A	B	L	E
A		I		I		O		O		L		E
D	E	B	U	G		W	O	R	R	I	E	D
I		E		I		S		A		G		E
R	A	S	H	L	Y		U	N	S	H	O	D

6

			E	M	B	E	L	L	I	S	H
W		H		N		E		A		N		O
E	X	A	C	T		L	O	W	D	O	W	N
S		U		R		I		N		T		E
T	A	T	T	E	R	E	D		W	H	E	Y
V		E		A		F		C		E		T
I	N	C	I	T	E		T	H	U	R	S	O
R		O		Y		T		E		W		N
G	L	U	T		S	W	A	N	S	O	N	G
I		T		B		I		I		R		U
N	E	U	T	R	O	N		L	A	D	L	E
I		R		A		G		L		S		D
A	C	E	T	Y	L	E	N	E			

7

	B	O	I	S	T	E	R	O	U	S
L		U		B		E		E		R
A	R	R	A	I	G	N		S	Q	U	I	B
R		N		S		N		I		G		U
Y	E	T	I		W	I	N	D	S	U	R	F
N			C		S		E		A		F
G	A	U	C	H	O		E	N	Z	Y	M	E
I		P		I		H		T			R
T	H	R	A	L	D	O	M		F	U	Z	Z
I		I		D		W		O		R		O
S	A	V	E	R		D	U	S	T	B	I	N
		E		E		A		L		A		E
	F	R	E	N	C	H	H	O	R	N	

8

D	E	C	E	I	T	F	U	L	N	E	S	S
E		A		N		A		U		N		P
P	A	L		S	A	T	I	R	I	C	A	L
O		L		E		H		E		O		A
T	W	I	T	C	H	E	R		B	U	O	Y
		S		R		R		E		R		E
S	E	T	T	E	E		O	N	W	A	R	D
C		H		T		F		S		G		
A	X	E	L		B	U	T	C	H	E	R	S
R		N		P		S		O		M		E
P	R	I	V	A	T	I	O	N		E	W	E
E		C		L		O		C		N		D
R	E	S	P	L	E	N	D	E	N	T	L	Y

9

D	E	C	A	D	E		C	R	O	P	U	P
E		H		W		T		U		R		A
S	P	A	N	I	S	H		S	C	O	T	T
A		N		N		O		K		P		T
D	A	T	E	D		M	I	S	T	A	K	E
E				L		A				N		R
	A	C	C	E	S	S	O	R	I	E	S	
E		H				H		E				G
G	R	E	N	A	D	A		C	A	B	A	L
R		R		S		R		L		R		I
E	L	I	O	T		D	E	I	F	I	E	D
S		S		I		Y		N		L		E
S	P	H	E	R	E		G	E	L	L	E	R

10

		S	I	M	I	L	A	R	I	T	Y	
A		H		A		E		O		E		
P	L	A	U	D	I	T		T	I	M	I	D
O		R		E		R		A		P		E
L	U	D	O		D	I	C	T	A	T	O	R
O			M		P		I		E		O	
G	E	N	I	A	L		H	O	T	D	O	G
I		O		N		G		N				A
S	Q	U	A	D	R	O	N		F	A	C	T
E		R		O		G		C		D		O
D	R	I	L	L		G	O	U	N	D	E	R
		S		I		L		L		E		Y
	C	H	A	N	C	E	L	L	O	R		

11

			P	U	S	H	A	H	E	A	D	
W		L		A		P	R		X		I	
H	O	O	K	S		A	C	C	E	P	T	S
O		O		S		R		H		E		H
L	I	K	E	W	I	S	E		U	R	G	E
E		I		O		E		F		I		A
H	U	N	G	R	Y		P	R	I	M	E	R
E		G		D		C		U		E		T
A	R	G	O		V	A	R	I	A	N	C	E
R		L		J		R		T		T		N
T	R	A	D	U	C	E		F	R	A	M	E
E		S		N		S		U		L		D
D	I	S	P	E	R	S	A	L				

12

G	E	R	M	A	N	M	E	A	S	L	E	S
U		E		R		I		L		I		I
T	O	P	I	C	A	L		C	I	T	E	D
		L		H		D		A		H		E
B	R	I	M		R	E	S	T	L	E	S	S
O		C		T		W		R				T
D	E	A	C	O	N		J	A	N	G	L	E
Y		B		I		Z		O		O		P
G	E	T	R	O	U	N	D		B	U	Y	S
U		O		G		H		C		R		
A	L	O	N	G		A	S	H	A	M	E	D
R		L		A		L		A		E		U
D	I	S	I	N	T	E	G	R	A	T	E	D

SOLUTIONS

13

N	O	N	S	E	N	S	E	V	E	R	S	E
	U		H		E		B		G		H	
S	T	A	R		G	E	O	R	G	I	A	N
	M		U		L		N		E			G
G	O	G	G	L	E	E	Y	E	D			
	D				C				O		J	
B	E	D	S	I	T		D	E	N	I	A	L
	D		C			E					C	
		A	D	M	I	R	A	T	I	O	N	
	F		L		U		I		I		B	
D	I	S	P	O	S	E	D		B	O	I	L
	V		E		E		E		E		T	
W	E	L	L	P	R	E	S	E	R	V	E	D

14

R	A	V	I	S	H		A	Z	O	R	E	S
E		A		A				A		U		T
C	O	R	F	U		A	R	M	E	N	I	A
I		I		N		R		B		U		P
P	R	O	R	A	T	A		E	X	P	E	L
E		U		B		Z						E
		S	I	M	P	E	R	I	N	G		
S			I		S			U		U		S
L	O	T	U	S		Q	U	A	R	T	E	T
I		V		S		U		G		L		A
V	E	S	T	I	G	E		A	P	E	R	Y
E		E		O				T		S		E
R	A	T	I	N	G		T	E	A	S	E	R

15

W	I	N	N	I	E	T	H	E	P	O	O	H
	N		I		X		E		A			I
L	U	N	G		P	E	N	I	T	E	N	T
	N		E		R		N		I			K
A	D	U	L	T	E	R	A	T	E			
	A		S						N		P	
S	T	U	M	P	S		R	E	T	O	R	T
	E		A		A		A				O	
		R	E	C	O	M	P	E	N	S	E	
	F		G		L		A		E		E	
V	A	G	A	B	O	N	D		J	O	C	K
	R		T		G		A		I		C	
I	M	P	E	R	S	O	N	A	T	I	O	N

16

C	A	P	T	O	R		P	R	I	M	A	L
U		U		F		B		I		A		A
D	U	T	I	F	U	L		L	U	R	K	S
D		O		B		A		E		Q		H
L	A	N	C	E		C	O	S	T	U	M	E
E				A		K				E		D
	C	A	S	T	E	L	L	A	T	E	D	
S		E		I		T				R		R
P	E	R	H	A	P	S		T	E	N	C	H
A		O		S		T		R		O		O
R	I	S	K	Y		E	X	A	L	T	E	D
E		O		E		D		C		E		E
D	I	L	A	T	E		A	T	O	D	D	S

17

W	A	S	P		K	R	A	K	A	T	O	A
R		Q		F		H		I		S		B
E	Q	U	E	R	R	Y		T	R	U	C	E
C		I		E		T		T		N		D
C	A	D	G	E		H	E	Y	D	A	Y	
H				Z		M				M		S
E	X	P	R	E	S	S	I	O	N	I	S	T
D		A			E		X					A
	C	L	I	N	I	C		F	L	U	N	G
B		A		I		T		O		S		E
R	E	V	U	P		I	N	R	O	A	D	S
O		E		P		O		D		G		E
W	O	R	R	Y	I	N	G		J	E	S	T

18

	S	K	A	T	E	B	O	A	R	D	E	R
B		N		E		A		P		R		E
R	I	O	J	A		R	E	P	R	O	O	F
A		C		T		K		L		N		R
I	C	K	Y		B	E	R	I	B	E	R	I
N		E		C		R		Q				G
W	O	R	T	H	Y		J	U	N	G	L	E
A				E		P		E		R		R
S	E	C	O	N	D	L	Y		P	I	S	A
H		R		I		A		E		S		T
I	D	E	A	L	L	Y		D	I	T	T	O
N		D		L		E		I		L		R
G	L	O	B	E	T	R	O	T	T	E	R	

19

M	O	D	I	C	U	M		O		R		G
O		I		O		E	N	R	O	U	T	E
S	H	A	N	N	O	N		N		B		N
E		R		S		D	R	A	G	O	U	T
S	T	Y	L	E		E		M		U		L
	A			C	U	R	R	E	N	T	L	Y
	K			U				N			I	
H	E	A	R	T	F	E	L	T			V	
I		T		I		R		A	S	S	E	S
P	A	L	A	V	E	R		T		T		T
P		A		E		O	R	I	N	O	C	O
I	N	S	U	L	A	R		O		O		U
E		T		Y		S	I	N	G	L	E	T

20

P	H	Y	S	I	C	I	A	N		H		I
	A		A		A		N		C	O	O	L
P	R	I	V	I	L	E	G	E		M		L
	P		E		M		O		V	I	V	A
A		S		C	E	L	L	S		C		T
U	N	T	O	L	D		A	C	T	I	V	E
T		A		I				O		D		A
O	U	T	I	N	G		M	U	R	A	L	S
C		E		G	R	O	A	T		L		E
R	A	M	P		O		R		F		S	
A		E		O	V	E	R	B	L	O	W	N
C	E	N	T		E		E		A		A	
Y		T		G	L	A	D	S	T	O	N	E

SOLUTIONS

21

22

23

24

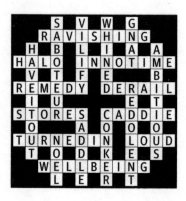

25

26

27

28

SOLUTIONS

29

			M	O	U	T	H	W	A	S	H
B		H	O		P		A		B		I
A	P	A	R	T		B	I	L	T	O	N	G
C		S	O		E		F		V		H
O	U	T	B	R	E	A	K		W	E	L	L
N		A		I		T		U		A		Y
A	I	L	I	N	G		A	N	K	L	E	S
N		A		G		S		S		L		T
D	I	V	A		F	O	R	E	B	E	A	R
E		I		S		U		E		L		U
G	O	S	L	I	N	G		M	A	S	O	N
G		T		N		H		L		E		G
S	E	A	W	O	R	T	H	Y			

30

B	R	O	O	K	S		A	V	O	W	A	L
E		M		Y			E		H		A
G	R	I	L	L		T	E	R	R	I	F	Y
O		C		I		E		B		S		E
F	O	R	B	E	A	R		O	U	T	E	R
F		O			M		S					S
	N	E	G	L	I	G	E	N	T		
L			O		N		N		W		M
I	N	T	R	O		A	I	R	L	I	N	E
E		A		D		T		A		N		D
D	U	R	A	B	L	E		P	O	K	E	D
E		N		Y			I		L		L
R	U	S	S	E	T		A	D	H	E	R	E

31

R	A	P	T		B	A	C	C	A	R	A	T
E		R		W		S		R		E		A
S	M	O	T	H	E	R		O	F	F	E	R
E		W		E		I		W		R		T
M	E	L	E	E		G	E	N	D	E	R	
B			Z		H				S		S
L	E	A	V	E	I	T	A	T	T	H	A	T
E		R		A		H			A			A
	S	T	U	M	P	S		R	I	V	E	R
S		L		E		R		I		E		K
I	N	E	P	T		A	D	V	E	R	S	E
G		S		A		I		E		S		R
H	U	S	T	L	I	N	G		D	O	S	S

32

F	U	C	H	S	I	A		B		G		A
R		L		H		P	U	L	L	O	U	T
A	V	O	C	A	D	O		O		D		T
N		W		D		L	E	O	N	I	N	E
K	E	N	D	O		L		D		V		S
	V			W	O	O	D	C	R	A	F	T
	I		C			U				A	
A	L	A	B	A	S	T	E	R			K
S		W		B		O		D	E	T	E	R
P	O	N	T	I	F	F		L		R		I
E		I		N		F	A	I	L	I	N	G
C	O	N	C	E	D	E		N		T		I
T		G		T		E	G	G	H	E	A	D

33

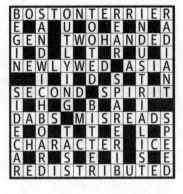

34

35

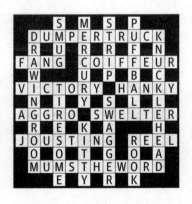

36

SOLUTIONS

37

38

39

40

41

```
. . . . B A B Y G R A N D
T W . A . A . R . . T . O
H E A R D . S P A N D A U
E . T . M . K . F . E . B
C H E R O K E E . D A H L
A . R . U . T . H . T . E
R E B A T E . C O S H E D
E . O . H . O . R . S . E
T O A D . S P O R A D I C
A . T . G . I . I . O . K
K A M P A L A . B O O N E
E . A . R . T . L . R . R
R U N N Y M E D E . . . .
```

42

```
B U T T E R M I L K . . .
. E . E . A . I . O . M .
T E N N Y S O N . C H I C
. C . T . Y . O . U . N .
H O P E . G R E M L I N .
. . E . C . K . . . . O .
L E G E R D E M A I N . .
A . . . U . Y . . I . . .
B R E V I T Y . B R U M .
D . I . C . A . S . I . .
G O E R . H U S H H U S H
N . G . E . B . I . E . .
. G O B S T O P P E R . .
```

43

```
D A C E . S T A R T L E D
I . R . S . U . O . A . E
S C O O T E R . O F T E N
A . N . R . N . M . E . T
R H Y M E . A B S U R D .
R . . A . B . . . O . U .
A S L I K E L Y A S N O T
Y . I . . I . P . . . I .
. U N I S O N . P E A R L
B . C . H . D . E . L . I
L A T H E . E N A B L E S
E . U . E . Y . L . O . E
D I S C R E E T . O W E D
```

44

```
W A R D R O B E . A C T S
O . E . I . I . C . E . C
M A G I C . S P O I L E R
B . E . H . E . L . E . E
. I N C A L C U L A B L E
C . C . R . T . Y . . . C
R I Y A D H . T W I T C H
I . . N . B . O . E . Y .
B I L L I A R D B A L L .
B . I . X . O . B . L . N
A N D S O O N . L D O P A
G . O . N . C . E . F . V
E A S T . H O R S E F L Y
```

SOLUTIONS

45

```
F A S H I O N V I C T I M
  M   A   P   O   R   R
S P I V   T E D D Y B O Y
  H   O   I   K   P   N
W I T C H C R A F T   I
  B   A   A   I   C
M I S S A L   V E C T O R
  A   I   O       O   N
      B O T T L E N E C K
  S   L   A   C   Y   R
E T H I O P I A   L I E D
  Y   N   E   N   O   T
G E I G E R C O U N T E R
```

46

```
          N E R V E L E S S
S   S   O   E   A   V   T
L A T E R   V E R B O S E
U   O   T   I   S   L   A
M U R P H I E S   M U L L
B   M   E   W   S   T   T
E X T O R T   M U N I C H
R   R   N   M   B   O   E
P R O P   H U S T I N G S
A   O   L   E   I   A   H
R E P R E S S   T O R S O
T   E   E   L   L   Y   W
Y O R K S H I R E
```

47

```
  A B B E S S   R E C U R
  V   A   A   E   A   E
H E A D O N   G I B B E T
  R   D   D   N   I   A
S T Y E   H E L S I N K I
  E   B   U   O   E   L
  D E T E R I O R A T E
A   L   S   K   L   X
C U L O T T E S   L O P E
C   I   Y   M   U   E
E X P O S E   A R D E N T
S   S   O   R   E   S
S H E E N   S T O D G E
```

48

```
L A C K A D A I S I C A L
I   U   Q   D   O   O   O
B A R   U N A S H A M E D
R   T   A   P   O   M   G
A L A C R I T Y   M I R E
    I   I   S   D   S   R
S I N F U L   R E V E L S
C   R   M   T   T   R
R E A P   S H O R T A G E
A   I   L   R   I   T   R
T E S T A M E N T   I R E
C   E   N   S   U   O   C
H O R S E C H E S T N U T
```

49

50

51

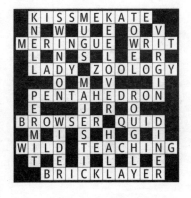

52

SOLUTIONS

53

54

55

56

57

```
  P E R F E C T P I T C H
A M   R   E   A   R   I
P R I D E   D A S H I N G
P   N   T   A   H   B   H
R E E K   C R O M W E L L
O   N   P   S   I       A
A U T H O R   U N S E E N
C     W   F   A   M   D
H E R M E T I C   S O A P
A   A   R   T   L   T   O
B E N E F I T   A R I A N
L   C   U   E   S   O   Y
E X H I L A R A T I N G
```

58

59

60

SOLUTIONS

61

62

63

64

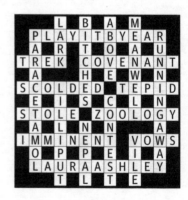

65

66

67

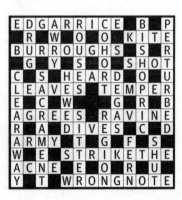

68

SOLUTIONS

69

	M	E	N	D	E	L	S	S	O	H	N	
S		R		E		A		P		O		T
C	O	A	L	M	I	N	E	R		B	O	O
I			O		C		I		G			A
S	P	O	O	N		E	N	G	R	O	S	S
S		F		I		T			B			T
O	F	F	I	C	E		V	E	L	L	U	M
R		C			U		X		I			A
K	N	O	C	K	O	N		T	O	N	G	S
I		L		E		C		I				T
C	O	O		B	R	O	W	N	R	I	C	E
K		U		A		O		C		D		R
	T	R	I	B	U	L	A	T	I	O	N	

70

D	R	I	B	S	A	N	D	D	R	A	B	S
E		N		U		O		I		U		E
N	O	T		F	L	U	M	M	O	X	E	D
I		E		F		G		E		I		A
M	A	R	Z	I	P	A	N		C	L	O	T
		P		C		T		B		I		E
B	R	E	W	E	R		A	L	W	A	Y	S
O		R		S		J		E		R		
R	I	S	K		C	A	T	S	E	Y	E	S
E		O		A		R		S		V		H
D	U	N	E	B	U	G	G	Y		E	A	R
O		A		L		O		O		R		U
M	I	L	L	E	N	N	I	U	M	B	U	G

71

B	O	A	T		F	O	L	L	O	W	E	R
E		B			R		A		A		E	
N	O	S	H		T	I	A	M	A	R	I	A
G		O		L		O		E		T		D
H	O	L	Y	I	S	L	A	N	D			
A		U		K		E		T		M		H
Z	I	T	H	E	R		G	A	L	A	X	Y
I		E		L		I		B		C		S
			L	I	O	N	E	L	B	A	R	T
P		F		H		D		E		R		E
O	N	L	O	O	K	E	R		R	O	A	R
U		A		O		N			N			I
R	I	G	I	D	I	T	Y		V	I	S	A

72

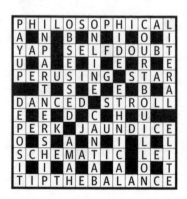

P	H	I	L	O	S	O	P	H	I	C	A	L
A		N		B		N		I		O		I
Y	A	P		S	E	L	F	D	O	U	B	T
U		A		E		I		E		R		E
P	E	R	U	S	I	N	G		S	T	A	R
		T		S		E		E		B		A
D	A	N	C	E	D		S	T	R	O	L	L
E		E		D		C		H		U		
P	E	R	K		J	A	U	N	D	I	C	E
O		S		A		N		I		L		L
S	C	H	E	M	A	T	I	C		L	E	I
I		I		A		A		A		O		T
T	I	P	T	H	E	B	A	L	A	N	C	E

73

			S	O	F	T	T	O	U	C	H
M	B	E		R		R		N		A	
A	L	L	I	N		O	V	A	T	I	O	N
K		A	I		S		P		M		G
E	S	C	A	L	A	T	E		C	A	R	T
T		K	I		Y		R		G		O
H	A	B	I	T	S		S	E	E	I	N	G
E		E	Y		C		S		N		E
G	E	R	M		T	A	K	E	P	A	R	T
R		R	C		N		R		B		H
A	L	I	M	O	N	Y		V	A	L	U	E
D		E	I		O		E		E		R
E	N	S	H	R	I	N	E	D

74

B	E	Y	O	N	D	M	E	A	S	U	R	E
	L		K		O		M		P		A
B	E	T	A		S	U	B	U	R	B	I	A
	V		P		S		E		A		D
F	A	M	I	L	I	A	R	L	Y
	T			E			E		C
H	O	O	V	E	R		E	A	R	N	E	R
	R		I		N				L
		S	A	N	D	C	A	S	T	L	E
	P	I		O		H	E	M
P	L	E	T	H	O	R	A		P	R	A	Y
	E	E	S		N		I		T
P	A	D	D	L	E	S	T	E	A	M	E	R

75

	T	H	E	B	E	E	S	K	N	E	E	S
E		A	O		S		E		J		I
N	I	N	N	Y		C	A	N	T	E	E	N
T		S	S		O		K		C		G
H	E	A	L		O	R	I	E	N	T	A	L
U		R	F		T		S		E
S	O	D	D	E	N		B	E	C	A	L	M
I		L		G		Y		T		I
A	N	A	L	O	G	U	E		C	A	E	N
S		D	D		S	G	L	D
T	E	M	P	E	S	T		A	T	O	N	E
I		I	S		A	I		S		D
C	O	N	S	E	R	V	A	T	I	S	M

76

S	H	U	N		D	I	D	A	C	T	I	C
T		N		N		P		O			A
E	W	E	S		S	T	R	I	P	O	F	F
A		A	B		E		C		K		E
D	I	S	D	A	I	N	F	U	L
I		I	N		D		L		S		F
E	C	L	A	I	R		U	T	O	P	I	A
R		Y		S		P	U		L	D
			C	H	A	R	T	R	E	U	S	E
I		B		M	O		E		T		A
B	A	R	B	E	C	U	E		S	T	E	W
I		A		N		S			E		A
S	P	E	C	T	A	T	E		F	R	A	Y

SOLUTIONS

77

M	I	D	D	L	E	S	B	R	O	U	G	H
	M		O		L		E		N		E	
A	M	I	D		D	O	N	E	T	H	A	T
	I		G		E		I		H		R	
A	N	N	E	B	R	O	N	T	E			
	E		L				G		G		C	
O	N	E	W	A	Y		P	H	O	B	O	S
	T		H		A				N		N	
	J		I	M	M	O	D	E	R	A	T	E
	J		T		A		S		A		I	
P	U	G	I	L	I	S	T		K	A	N	E
	D		N		Z		O		E		U	
T	O	N	G	U	E	T	W	I	S	T	E	R

78

C	L	I	M	B	D	O	W	N		E		W
	I		O		I		I		H	A	Z	E
E	N	C	L	O	S	U	R	E		V		L
	T		E		M		I		P	E	E	L
S		A		F	A	I	N	T		S		T
P	L	U	R	A	L		G	A	N	D	E	R
I		S		D				S		R		I
N	A	T	T	E	R		S	T	R	O	K	E
D		E		D	E	C	A	Y		P		D
R	A	R	E		B		D		M		F	
I		I		Q	U	A	D	R	U	P	E	D
F	A	T	E		K		E		S		N	
T		Y		B	E	A	N	F	E	A	S	T

79

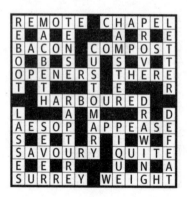

R	E	M	O	T	E		C	H	A	P	E	L
E		A		E			A		R		E	
B	A	C	O	N		C	O	M	P	O	S	T
O		B		S		U		S		V		T
O	P	E	N	E	R	S		T	H	E	R	E
T		T		T		T		E				R
		H	A	R	B	O	U	R	E	D		
L			A		M			R		D	
A	E	S	O	P		A	P	P	E	A	S	E
S		E		T		R		I		W		F
S	A	V	O	U	R	Y		Q	U	I	T	E
E		E		R				U		N		A
S	U	R	R	E	Y		W	E	I	G	H	T

80

G	R	A	V	I	T	A	T	E		J		S
	A		A		O		U		V	E	T	O
I	T	I	N	E	R	A	R	Y		L		V
	E		E		Q		N		B	L	U	E
C		A		R	U	L	E	R		Y		R
A	U	N	T	I	E		R	U	M	B	L	E
R		N		V				P		A		I
P	R	O	Z	A	C		B	E	D	B	U	G
E		U		L	O	I	R	E		Y		N
T	U	N	E		P		E		D		B	
B		C		C	O	T	E	D	A	Z	U	R
A	G	E	S		U		Z		U		R	
G		R		S	T	E	E	L	B	A	N	D

81

```
  D U S S E L D O R F
S   O   O   M   R   O
H E N C O O P   O A S I S
E   O   T   L   P   E   N
E U R O   C O C K A T O O
P       N   Y   I   T   W
S U B D U E   S C R E A M
H   O   T   S   K       O
A Q U A R I U S   S W A B
N   D   I   M   U   A   I
K R O N E   M A G I C A L
    I   N   E   L   K   E
  F R A T E R N I T Y
```

82

```
      B   S   S   S
  E L A S T I C A T E D
  Q   R   U   A   A   I
P U N K   M A R Y L A N D
I   I   P   F   L   I
C L O T H E S   P I N N Y
I   I   E   D   U   O   G
A B Y S S   I N A N I T Y
R   R   T   P   H       A
L I S T E R I A   C U B E
U   U   U   O   P   R   L
M O B I L E P H O N E
    E   E   Y   P
```

83

```
    D   S C   H
  D O G C O L L A R
W   C   A   O   W   I
D I E U   T A S H K E N T
T   S   T   E       F
C H O O S Y   T I P P L E
S   A       O   U
S T A P L E   P A U S E D
A   X   E   L   N
I N N O C E N T   T A C K
D   R   M   I   I   E
  S L A P S T I C K
  Y   T   E   E
```

84

```
  O V E R W H E L M I N G
B   I   A   O   I   M   L
L A S E R   B U F F A L O
A   C   E   A   E   G   C
C L E F   F R E T W O R K
K   R   E   T   I       E
P L A Q U E   A M A Z O N
U   R   T   E   I   S
D E S P O T I C   S L I P
D   T   S   N   I   L   I
I D I O T I C   N O I S E
N   N   A   A   C   O   L
G U T W R E N C H I N G
```

SOLUTIONS

85

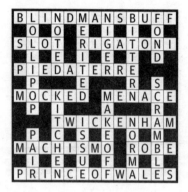

86

87

88

89

90

91

92

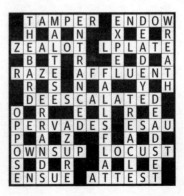

SOLUTIONS

93

94

95

96

97

S	C	H	A	D	E	N	F	R	E	U	D	E
T		O		E		I		O		N		Y
R	U	B		L	A	N	D	S	L	I	D	E
A		S		I		E		E		M		S
W	O	O	D	C	U	T	S		S	A	G	O
		N		A		Y		B		G		R
A	L	S	A	C	E		V	I	R	I	L	E
C		C		Y		G		R		N		
E	C	H	O		Q	U	A	D	R	A	N	T
R		O		B		N		B		T		H
B	R	I	T	A	N	N	I	A		I	C	Y
I		C		R		E		T		V		M
C	H	E	D	D	A	R	C	H	E	E	S	E

98

H	I	K	E		S	N	U	G	G	L	E	S
O		A		K		O		R		A		U
R	E	F	L	E	C	T		A	S	S	A	M
N		K		T		O		S		T		P
P	L	A	N	T		N	A	P	K	I	N	
I			L		Y			Y			N	S
P	I	E	C	E	S	O	F	E	I	G	H	T
E		C			U		X				A	
	B	U	R	S	A	R		C	I	D	E	R
A		A		C		L		U		I		T
V	O	D	K	A		I	N	S	P	A	T	E
O		O		R		F		E		N		R
N	O	R	S	E	M	E	N		N	A	B	S

99

S	P	E	C	I	A	L	B	R	A	N	C	H
C		L		N		I		O		E		O
U	S	E		S	P	E	E	D	D	I	A	L
B		C		T		L		S		G		I
A	C	T	U	A	T	O	R		S	H	A	D
		R		N		W		D		B		A
S	W	I	T	C	H		M	E	M	O	R	Y
P		C		E		T		R		U		
O	R	C	A		C	H	A	R	T	R	E	S
U		H		K		R		I		H		C
S	T	A	B	I	L	I	S	E		O	V	A
E		I		E		F		R		O		R
S	H	R	O	V	E	T	U	E	S	D	A	Y

100

F	L	O	A	T	I	N	G	V	O	T	E	R
E		P		A		A		E		H		O
D	R	E	A	M	U	P		H	O	O	E	Y
		R		E		E		E		R		A
B	R	A	Y		C	R	I	M	I	N	A	L
A		T		L		Y		E				B
R	E	E	F	E	R		E	N	A	M	E	L
O			T		C		T		A		U	
F	I	S	H	H	O	O	K		I	S	L	E
S		A		A		P		C		T		
O	T	T	E	R		P	R	O	V	I	S	O
A		I		G		E		L		F		W
P	E	N	N	Y	D	R	E	A	D	F	U	L

SOLUTIONS

101

R	A	P	P	R	O	C	H	E	M	E	N	T
R		A		O		A		M		L		A
M	I	D	T	O	W	N		P	R	A	N	K
		D		F		A		H		T		E
A	L	O	T		A	D	J	A	C	E	N	T
R		C		U		A		T				U
B	A	K	I	N	G		L	I	M	B	E	R
O				C		T		C		O		N
R	A	B	E	L	A	I	S		H	O	P	S
E		L		E		M		B		K		
T	E	A	R	S		B	E	A	M	I	N	G
U		S		A		E		C		E		A
M	E	T	A	M	O	R	P	H	O	S	I	S

102

L	A	B	O	U	R		G	E	R	B	I	L
A		A		T			X		E			U
T	W	I	S	T		G	E	A	R	B	O	X
E		L		E		O		M		O		U
S	T	I	R	R	E	D		P	A	P	E	R
T		F			F		L					Y
		F	I	R	M	A	M	E	N	T		
G			E			T			W		A	
O	C	T	A	L		H	U	S	B	A	N	D
S		R		A		E		T		D		V
S	L	E	E	P	E	R		I	N	D	I	E
I			N		S			L		L		R
P	O	T	T	E	R		F	L	U	E	N	T

103

		S		S		C		W				
	N	A	M	E	C	A	L	L	I	N	G	
	U		U		A		E		N		O	
S	P	I	T		T	R	A	P	D	O	O	R
	T				T		R		D		D	
N	I	B	B	L	E	S		R	O	U	N	D
	A		O		R		G		W		A	
A	L	O	U	D		T	R	I	N	I	T	Y
	M		L		S		I		I		U	
D	A	Y	D	R	E	A	M		F	O	R	K
	S		E		I		S		O		E	
S	P	R	I	N	G	B	O	A	R	D		
		S		E		Y		L				

104

I	N	T	H	E	D	O	G	H	O	U	S	E
	O		E		I		R		N		O	
E	T	N	A		C	H	A	S	T	I	T	Y
A		V		K		V		H			S	
T	H	E	E	V	I	L	E	Y	E			
O				E			E		G		F	
S	P	A	S	M	S		E	X	O	D	U	S
E		P			X				G			
		L	A	W	N	T	E	N	N	I	S	
Y		I		E		R		A		T		
F	O	R	C	I	B	L	E		D	R	I	P
K		E		E		M		I		V		
T	E	N	D	E	R	H	E	A	R	T	E	D

105

Grid 105:

```
P L A Y . S P R I N G U P
A . L . . O . M . U . U
C A L L . C L E M A T I S
I . I . W . A . S . . H
F R A T E R N I T Y . . .
I . N . L . D . E . I . P
S I C I L Y . C R O M E R
T . E . I . C . I . M . A
. . . U N P L E A S A N T
J . S . G . O . L . T . T
E L E C T I V E . P U L L
E . M . O . E . . . R . E
P O I G N A N T . L E W D
```

106

Grid 106:

```
C A T T L E S T A T I O N
L . R . E . A . P . M . E
A L I . G U I N E A P I G
S . A . S . G . D . R . A
S O L U T I O N . H A L T
. A . U . N . F . C . E
P A N A M A . S I F T E D
R . D . P . M . D . I
O M E N . H A N D I C A P
P . R . N . P . L . A . U
H A R P E R L E E . B O P
E . O . M . E . R . L . I
T O R T O I S E S H E L L
```

107

Grid 107:

```
. . T . T . G . D . . . .
. C U R R Y F A V O U R .
. H . I . P . U . U . O .
W A R P . H I G H B A L L
. R . . . O . E . T . L .
G L A S G O W . A F F I X
. E . T . N . P . U . N .
O S C A R . T R I L O G Y
. L . N . C . E . . . I .
H A N D T O O L . R U N G
. M . I . U . U . . . A .
. B I N A R Y D I G I T .
. . G . T . E . E . . . .
```

108

Grid 108:

```
. . . F . N . Q . L . . .
. M O L E C U L A R . . .
. T . U . R . O . W . S .
F E A R . V E R O N I C A
R . T . E . U . . . A . A
B R I E F S . M U T A T E
. I . E . . . . . E . T .
S T O N E S . D I E T E R
. O . . K . E . N . R .
F R E A K O U T . A P E X
. Y . L . P . A . G . D
. . C A R J A C K E R .
. . . S . E . H . R . .
```

259

SOLUTIONS

109

110

111

112

113

Grid solution:

FICKLENESS
O Y A O P M
PRECIOUS LOOT
T L S E I R
HOOK EGOTISM
N S A E
CHEEKBYJOWL
O I S A
HICCUPS DRAW
T U J G S E
RUMP ACRIMONY
S P C I E D
HANKYPANKY

114

SABBATH B U G
A O S ATLANTA
BRUISER A S N
R G A DONJUAN
ETHOS E D R E
H SENTIMENT
O I S O
BRAINWASH V
U S A N MIDAS
ROTATES E R E
R U I WINSOME
OUTDONE T S P
W E N RESISTS

115

JINGLE CLIPON
O O A E I E
SQUAD JITTERS
T R L U T C T
LOITERS IDEAL
E S T N E
HARBINGER
P E F E P
ACRID INORDER
S E W E B M I
SEAFOOD EVENS
U L O S A S
POMADE SENTRY

116

FLASHPOINT
L D O V O B
DELEGATE VARY
S P X R E E
HATE STILTED
L A U C
BEYONDREACH
A G N N
GRUMBLE SNOB
L A I B U A
KEEN CLUELESS
Y G A L A T
BYANDLARGE

SOLUTIONS

117

118

119

120

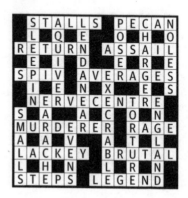

121

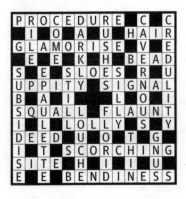

F	A	M	E		S	H	I	F	T	K	E	Y
F	O		E			I		A		I		O
O	A	T	H		V	A	G	R	A	N	C	Y
L		A		I		T		M		K		O
S	U	P	E	R	H	U	M	A	N			
C		H		R		S		N		S		B
A	T	O	M	I	C		V	I	R	T	U	E
P		R		G		N		M		I		G
		M	A	L	E	F	A	C	T	O	R	
L		Z		T		B		L		C		U
E	M	E	R	I	T	U	S		T	H	U	D
A		T		O		L			U			G
D	R	A	W	N	E	A	R		A	P	S	E

122

C	O	L	D	F	E	E	T		C	A	V	A
R		A		I		N		C		L		L
U	N	C	L	E		D	A	H	L	I	A	S
X		T		L		I		E		B		A
	H	A	N	D	O	V	E	R	F	I	S	T
F		T		G		E		R				I
A	G	E	O	L	D		M	Y	O	P	I	A
C			A		K		B		O			N
T	R	A	N	S	M	O	G	R	I	F	Y	
O		N		S		S		A		A		L
T	A	N	G	E	L	O		N	I	C	H	E
U		I		S		V		D		E		F
M	E	E	K		C	O	P	Y	E	D	I	T

123

P	R	O	C	E	D	U	R	E		C		C
	I		O		A		U		H	A	I	R
G	L	A	M	O	R	I	S	E		V		E
	E		E		K		H		B	E	A	D
S		E		S	L	O	E	S		R		U
U	P	P	I	T	Y			S	I	G	N	A	L
B		A		I			L		O		I
S	Q	U	A	L	L		F	L	A	U	N	T
I		L		L	O	L	L	Y		S		Y
D	E	E	D		U		O		T		G
I		T		S	C	O	R	C	H	I	N	G
S	I	T	E		H		I		I		U
E		E		B	E	N	D	I	N	E	S	S

124

R	I	B	S		C	O	N	S	I	D	E	R
E		E		D		N		T		E		I
S	U	G	G	E	S	T		O	N	T	A	P
I		A		C		H		A		E		S
D	I	N	E	R		E	X	T	E	N	T	
U				E		F				T		S
A	T	T	H	E	E	A	R	L	I	E	S	T
L		A		C		A		A				U
	S	C	Y	T	H	E		D	E	B	A	R
J		T		U		O		I		O		G
U	N	F	E	D		F	I	N	E	S	S	E
S		U		O		I		G		S		O
T	O	L	E	R	A	T	E		C	Y	A	N

SOLUTIONS

125

126

127

128

129

130

131

132

SOLUTIONS

133

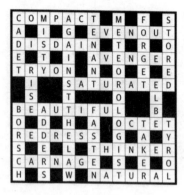

134

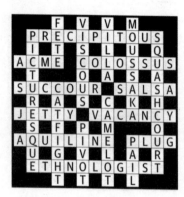

135

136

137

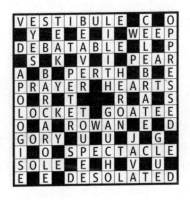

138

139

140

SOLUTIONS

141

142

143

144

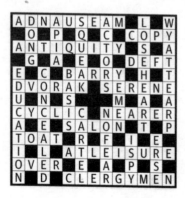

145

146

147

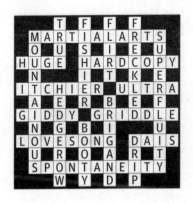

148

SOLUTIONS

149

150

151

152

153

```
  D R A W S T R I N G S
M   Y   R   W   C   I   P
O P E R A T I V E   F I R
N       N   T   U   T   O
S W I N G   C A P I T O L
T   N   L   H       O   E
R O C K E T   R A C K E T
O   A       S   R   E   A
S U R R E A L   S O N A R
I   N   N   I   E       I
T E A   A R G E N T I N A
Y   T   C   H   A   R   N
  T E E T O T A L L E R
```

154

155

156

SOLUTIONS

157

158

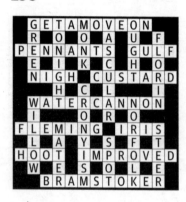

159

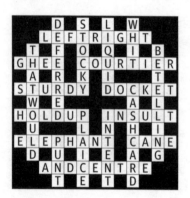

160

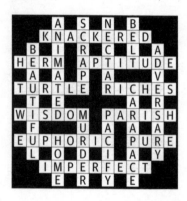

161

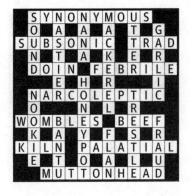

162

163

164

SOLUTIONS

165

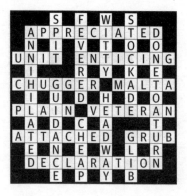

166

167

168

169

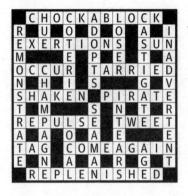

170

171

172

SOLUTIONS

173

174

175

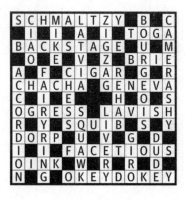

176

177

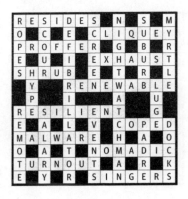

```
  O F F T H E R E C O R D
H   O   I   S   L   R   O
E R R E D   T R O D D E N
A   A   Y   E   N   E   K
R U G S   K E D G E R E E
T   E   B   M   A       Y
T A R T A N   E T H I C S
O       L   M   E   M   Y
H A M I L T O N   A P S E
E   U   C   S   W   I   A
A F F R O N T   A M O U R
R   T   C   L   L   U   S
T R I C K C Y C L I S T
```

178

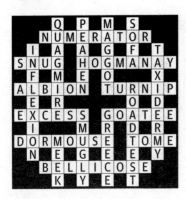

```
      Q   P   M   S
  N U M E R A T O R
  I   A   A   G   F   T
S N U G   H O G M A N A Y
  F   M   E   O       X
A L B I O N   T U R N I P
  E   R       O   D
E X C E S S   G O A T E E
  I       M   R   D   R
D O R M O U S E   T O M E
  N   E   G   E   E   Y
  B E L L I C O S E
  K   Y   E   T
```

179

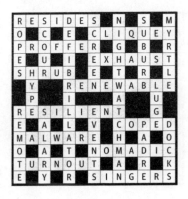

```
R E S I D E S   N   S   M
O   C   E   C L I Q U E Y
P R O F F E R   G   B   R
E   U   I   E X H A U S T
S H R U B   E   T   R   L
  Y       R E N E W A B L E
  P   I       A       U
R E S I L I E N T   G
E   A   L   V   C O P E D
M A L W A R E   H   A   O
O   A   T   N O M A D I C
T U R N O U T   A   R   K
E   Y   R   S I N G E R S
```

180

```
H O C K   S H O R E S U P
E   R   S   A   E   A   U
S T I M U L I   C A M E L
I   C   D   R   C   U   P
T O K Y O   S H E R R Y
A       K   P       A   I
T O N G U E L A S H I N G
E   E       I   O       N
  U P S H O T   M A T Z O
C   T   O   T   B   H   M
H A U N T   I S R A E L I
A   N   E   N   E   F   N
T H E O L O G Y   S T A Y
```

SOLUTIONS

181

B	O	S	C	A	S	T	L	E		M		H
	X		U		I		O		B	O	N	O
P	E	R	E	G	R	I	N	E		N		T
	N		S		I		G		B	O	U	T
C		M		Q	U	I	E	T		L		O
H	I	A	T	U	S		R	A	G	O	U	T
A		U		I				M		G		R
M	O	R	A	L	S		M	A	P	U	T	O
P		I		L	U	G	E	R		E		T
A	S	T	I		D		R		P		L	
G		I		M	O	N	I	T	O	R	E	D
N	O	U	N		K		N		O		I	
E		S		A	U	T	O	C	R	O	S	S

182

F	L	O	P		E	C	L	I	P	S	E	D
A		D				A		C		U		R
L	I	D	O		E	P	H	E	M	E	R	A
L		I		P		E		L		T		Y
D	U	T	C	H	T	R	E	A	T			
O		I		A		S		N		V		I
W	H	E	R	R	Y		A	D	R	I	A	N
N		S		M		U		E		R		V
			L	A	U	N	D	R	E	T	T	E
R		F		C		S		S		U		S
I	N	I	M	I	C	A	L		P	O	U	T
T		L		S		F				S		O
E	V	E	N	T	H	E	N		T	O	U	R

183

P	E	D	I	C	U	R	E		D	A	T	A
A		E		U		E		P		C		N
G	O	F	E	R		P	R	E	S	T	O	N
E		I		D		A		T		E		O
	A	L	L	S	A	I	N	T	S	D	A	Y
G		E		A		D		Y				I
A	I	D	I	N	G		J	O	R	D	A	N
Z		D		S		F		F		E		G
P	L	A	Y	W	I	T	H	F	I	R	E	
A		U		H		O		I		R		B
C	O	N	G	E	A	L		C	H	I	N	A
H		T		Y		E		E		C		R
O	U	S	T		U	N	B	R	O	K	E	N

184

A	B	J	E	C	T		T	H	E	S	I	S
M		A		R		M		A		W		P
B	U	S	H	I	D	O		S	C	O	W	L
U		O		M		U		T		L		A
S	I	N	U	S		N	E	E	D	L	E	S
H				O		T		E				H
	D	O	W	N	P	A	Y	M	E	N	T	
A		P				I		E				M
C	A	T	A	L	A	N		S	U	S	H	I
U		I		A		A		S		I		D
M	U	M	P	S		S	T	I	L	T	E	D
E		U		E		H		A		E		A
N	O	M	O	R	E		S	H	O	D	D	Y

185

186

187

188

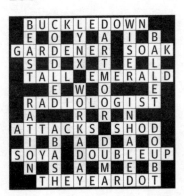

SOLUTIONS

189

190

191

192

193

D	U	C	T		S	T	A	R	C	H	E	D
E		I		P		E		I		O		E
W	A	V	E	R	E	R		S	A	U	C	E
I		I		O		P		E		S		R
N	Y	L	O	N		S	E	N	A	T	E	
E			T		I			O				S
S	H	A	D	O	W	C	A	B	I	N	E	T
S		T		H		E						I
	B	A	M	B	O	O		R	E	G	A	L
S		N		A		R		L		E		E
C	L	E	A	N		E	V	I	D	E	N	T
A		N		A				N		S		T
M	I	D	D	L	I	N	G		H	E	R	O

194

A	C	C	I	D	E	N	T	P	R	O	N	E
L		A		E		O		L		N		R
O	P	S		C	O	R	P	U	S	C	L	E
O		H		E		W		G		E		C
F	A	D	E	A	W	A	Y		C	U	L	T
		I		S		Y		N		P		E
P	I	S	C	E	S		H	A	R	O	L	D
A		P		D		T		R		N		
P	H	E	W		A	I	R	C	R	A	F	T
A		N		M		L		I		T		O
D	I	S	C	I	P	L	E	S		I	R	K
O		E		N		E		S		M		E
C	A	R	R	I	E	R	P	I	G	E	O	N

195

H	I	T	T	H	E	J	A	C	K	P	O	T
O		I		A		A		O		A		Y
P	A	P	Y	R	U	S		C	E	D	A	R
		P		K		P		K		D		A
D	I	L	L		V	E	R	A	L	Y	N	N
E		E		C		R		T				N
F	U	R	R	O	W		M	O	N	A	C	O
R				R		H		O		U		U
A	C	T	I	N	I	U	M		A	G	E	S
U		R		E		S		G		M		
D	R	A	W	L		H	A	U	T	E	U	R
E		I		I		E		R		N		O
D	O	N	E	A	N	D	D	U	S	T	E	D

196

G	L	A	S	S	E	S		R		M		B
U		D		I		K	N	O	W	A	L	L
S	W	I	N	D	L	E		O		T		I
T		O		E		W	E	T	S	U	I	T
O	A	S	I	S		E		V		R		H
	G			P	E	R	S	E	V	E	R	E
	R			L		G				E		
C	A	N	D	I	D	A	T	E		S		
O		I		T		R		T	I	L	T	H
M	I	N	U	T	I	A		A		O		I
B		E		I		R	E	B	O	U	N	D
A	N	T	E	N	N	A		L		S		E
T		Y		G		T	H	E	S	E	U	S

SOLUTIONS

197

198

199

200

201

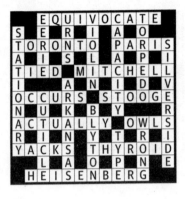

202

203

204

SOLUTIONS

205

206

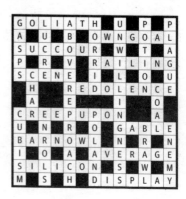

207

208

209

210

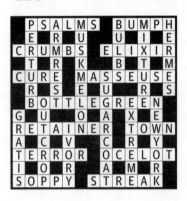

211

212

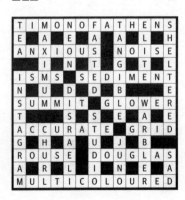

SOLUTIONS

213

214

215

216

217

```
  M A K E O N E S M A R K
F   T   L     U   O   D   N
A D L I B   B U F F A L O
C   E   A   I   T   G   W
E L A N   O L D S W E A T
T   S   R   E   O       H
H A T R E D   S A L U T E
E     B   T   P   P   R
M A R A U D E R   E R G O
U   U   T   M   V   O   P
S P L I T U P   A L O N E
I   E   A   T   I   T   S
C A R E L E S S N E S S
```

218

```
  G U L F O F M E X I C O
F   N   O   R   X   N   R
I N D E X   I M P L A N T
R   E   Y   D   E   N   H
E A R L   S A N D I E G O
M   G   M   Y   I       D
A N O R A K   S T E R E O
N       S   Z   E   E   N
S U M A T R A N   S T E T
L   U   O   G   B   I   I
I N S I D E R   L Y R I C
F   I   O   E   A   A   S
T E C H N O B A B B L E
```

219

```
  L U M B E R J A C K
E   I   I   N   U   O
F I N E L E G   M I R T H
F   K   D   I   B   O   E
R U S K   I N S O M N I A
O       R   E   J   E   V
N U M B E D   S E T T L E
T   E   U   G   T       N
E N D A N G E R   A W L S
R   I   I   E   A   O   E
Y E A S T   G A G A R I N
    T   E   E   E   D   T
  N E E D L E S S L Y
```

220

```
C L A S S E S   N   S   D
O   L   T   A P O S T L E
M A L L A R D   C   A   A
I   O   Y   D I L A T E D
C R Y P T   E   A   E   L
    H   H U R R I E D L Y
    E   E       M   O
C A P A C I O U S       N
L   R   O   G   B I K E R
U N U S U A L   O   A   A
M   N   R   I G N O R E D
S T E P S O N   U   M   O
Y   S   E   G A S M A I N
```

SOLUTIONS

221

222

```
P R I N C E E D W A R D
W E O X O T O
O R B I T P A R V E N U
R E E A M A B
L O C K I N F O R M A L
D C S D U E
W E A P O N I S L A N D
I N D E V E
D R E D G E R S Z I N C
E V B A B A K
W H I T I N G L A T T E
E T R O O O R
B O A R D I N G C A R D
```

```
D O W N C A S T M A I N
U E A P H L I
F E L O N E R O S I O N
F F T E U V E
B A L A N C E S H E E T
S R N H E E
C H E E K Y C O L L I E
A E W F E N
T O W E R H A M L E T S
H A O T O T B
I N D O U B T R O U T E
N E S L D C A
G O R Y M E S S D E C K
```

223

224

```
B U T T E R F I N G E R S
U U A O O B T
G E N E R A L L I B R A
N N L O E G
E W E S J O I N E D U P
D L L W G A
E U S T O N V E R G E R
L T U R E T
W A T C H I N G E S P Y
E A A J D T
I N N E R U N A W A R E
S G I S M P N
S T O W O N T H E W O L D
```

```
A D J U S T M E N T
R O A A O D
M I L L I N E R M E A L
E L E G A R
S H I N W I N D O W S
E L N I
F A S C I N A T I O N
L B L N
D A N G L E D M E W S
G E R D X A
S O F T A M E N A B L E
N O T E C A
I N T E G R A T E D
```